UNDERSTANDING THE EFFECT OF ELECTROMAGNETIC SIGNALS ON LIVING BEINGS

Rakesh Kumar

This book, Introduction to the Effect of Electromagnetic Signals on Living Beings, is dedicated to Vaiśeṣika, one of the six classical schools of Indian philosophy, which laid the foundation for the scientific understanding of nature, matter, and causality. Vaiśeṣika, founded by the sage Kaṇāda, is known for its atomic theory and detailed categorization of substances in the universe. This ancient school of thought deeply explored the nature of elements, motion, and interaction between material entities—ideas that resonate with modern scientific inquiries into electromagnetic fields and their effects on biological systems.

The philosophy of Vaiśeṣika, which classifies reality into categories such as Dravya (substance), Guṇa (quality), Karma (motion), Sāmānya (generality), Viśeṣa (particularity), and Samavāya (inherence), provides a structured approach to analyzing natural phenomena. It recognizes the presence of invisible forces that influence the physical world, much like the unseen but measurable impact of electromagnetic signals on living organisms.

By dedicating this book to Vaiśeṣika, we honor the timeless wisdom that sought to decode the mysteries of the natural world using observation, logic, and systematic classification. As modern research delves into the effects of electromagnetic radiation on human health, animal behavior, and environmental balance, we find a philosophical alignment with Vaiśeṣika's pursuit of knowledge. This book extends that tradition by exploring how invisible electromagnetic forces shape biological existence, bridging ancient insights with contemporary scientific advancements.

CONTENTS

INTRODUCTION

Electromagnetic radiation (EMR) surrounds us in our everyday lives, from the mobile phones we use to the Wi-Fi signals that keep us connected. Yet, while we are aware of its presence, the full extent of its effects on living beings—humans, animals, plants, and microorganisms—is still an area of ongoing research and debate. This book aims to provide an in-depth understanding of the influence of electromagnetic signals on living organisms, bridging the gap between ancient philosophical insights and modern scientific exploration.

The exploration of electromagnetic radiation is not new. In fact, even in the ancient Indian philosophical system of Vaiśeṣika, there were fundamental ideas about invisible forces and energies interacting with matter and living beings. As modern science has progressed, we now understand these forces more comprehensively, and the development of technologies like mobile phones, Wi-Fi routers, smart appliances, and medical devices has led to an increased exposure to electromagnetic fields. This rising exposure raises important questions about the potential biological effects of these EM signals on various forms of life.

In this book, we will delve into the different types of electromagnetic radiation, their propagation, and the biological mechanisms behind their interactions with living cells. We will explore both the short-term and long-term effects, the safety measures in place, and the public health concerns associated with these technologies. Additionally, we will consider the environmental impact, touching on how electromagnetic pollution could affect biodiversity and ecosystems.

As we move into an increasingly interconnected world, understanding the effects of electromagnetic radiation on living beings is essential. This book offers a comprehensive guide to the subject, examining both the scientific findings and the philosophical implications, ultimately aiming to provide readers with the knowledge needed to navigate the complexities of this invisible, yet ever-present, phenomenon.

WHAT ARE ELECTROMAGNETIC (EM) SIGNALS?

Electromagnetic (EM) signals are waves that carry energy through space and are composed of electric and magnetic fields oscillating perpendicular to each other. These waves travel at the speed of light and can propagate through a vacuum as well as through various mediums.

1. Basic Definition of EM Signals

Electromagnetic signals are fluctuations of electric and magnetic fields that move through space. These signals are generated naturally (e.g., sunlight, lightning) and artificially (e.g., radio waves, mobile phones, Wi-Fi, microwaves).

2. Components of an Electromagnetic Wave

An EM wave consists of two key components:

- **Electric Field (E):** A force field produced by electrically charged particles.

- **Magnetic Field (B):** A field created by moving electric charges.

- Both fields oscillate perpendicularly to each other and to the direction of wave propagation.

3. Properties of Electromagnetic Waves

- **Speed:** EM waves travel at the speed of light ($\approx$ 299,792 km/s in a vacuum).
- **Wavelength & Frequency:** These determine the type of EM wave.
  - **Wavelength (λ):** Distance between two peaks of a wave.
  - **Frequency (f):** Number of wave cycles per second (measured in Hertz, Hz).
- **Energy:** The energy of EM waves is proportional to their frequency (higher frequency = more energy).

4. Types of Electromagnetic Waves

The **Electromagnetic Spectrum** categorizes EM waves based on their frequency and wavelength:

Type of Wave	Frequency (Hz)	Wavelength (m)	Examples
Radio Waves	< 3 GHz	> 1 m	AM/FM Radio, Wi-Fi, TV Signals
Microwaves	3 GHz – 300 GHz	1 mm – 1 m	Microwave Ovens, Mobile Phones
Infrared (IR)	300 GHz – 400 THz	700 nm – 1 mm	Remote Controls, Thermal Imaging
Visible Light	400 THz – 700 THz	400 nm – 700 nm	Human Eye Perception
Ultraviolet (UV)	700 THz – 30 PHz	10 nm – 400 nm	Sunlight, Sterilization
X-Rays	30 PHz – 30 EHz	0.01 nm – 10 nm	Medical Imaging, Airport Security
Gamma Rays	> 30 EHz	< 0.01 nm	Nuclear Reactions, Cancer Treatment

(GHz: Gigahertz, THz: Terahertz, PHz: Petahertz, EHz: Exahertz, nm: nanometers, m: meters)

5. Sources of Electromagnetic Signals

Natural Sources:

- **Sunlight:** The most significant natural EM radiation source, covering UV, visible light, and infrared.
- **Lightning:** Produces radio waves and electromagnetic disturbances.
- **Earth's Magnetic Field:** Protects against harmful cosmic radiation.

Artificial Sources:

- **Radio and Television Broadcasting:** Uses radio waves for communication.
- **Mobile Phones and Wi-Fi:** Emit microwave frequencies for connectivity.
- **Medical Devices:** X-ray machines, MRI scanners use high-frequency EM waves.
- **Power Lines & Electrical Appliances:** Emit low-frequency electromagnetic fields (EMF).

6. How EM Signals Are Used in Communication

EM waves play a crucial role in modern communication:

- **Radio & TV Transmission:** Signals are modulated and transmitted via radio waves.
- **Mobile Networks & Wi-Fi:** Data is transmitted using microwaves and radio waves.
- **Satellite Communication:** Uses high-frequency waves to relay signals over long distances.

7. Importance and Risks of EM Signals

- **Benefits:**
  - Wireless communication and global connectivity.
  - Medical applications like imaging and diagnostics.
  - Scientific exploration and astronomical

research.

- **Potential Risks:**
    - High-energy EM waves (UV, X-rays, Gamma rays) can cause DNA damage.
    - Continuous exposure to artificial EM fields (mobile phones, Wi-Fi) raises concerns about long-term biological effects.

Conclusion

Electromagnetic signals are fundamental to both natural and technological processes. While they enable modern communication, healthcare, and scientific advancements, it is important to understand their interactions with living beings to mitigate potential risks.

TYPES OF ELECTROMAGNETIC RADIATION

Electromagnetic radiation (EMR) is classified based on its **wavelength** and **frequency** into different types, forming the **electromagnetic spectrum**. Each type has unique properties and applications.

1. The Electromagnetic Spectrum Overview

The EM spectrum consists of waves with varying frequencies and wavelengths. It ranges from low-energy **radio waves** to high-energy **gamma rays**.

Key Characteristics of Electromagnetic Waves:

- **Wavelength (λ):** Distance between two consecutive peaks or troughs of a wave (measured in meters).
- **Frequency (f):** Number of wave cycles per second (measured in Hertz, Hz).
- **Energy:** Higher frequency means higher energy, and vice versa.

Type of Radiation	Frequency Range	Wavelength Range	Energy Level
Radio Waves	< 3 GHz	> 1 m	Low
Microwaves	3 GHz – 300 GHz	1 mm – 1 m	Low
Infrared (IR)	300 GHz – 400	700 nm – 1 mm	Moderate

	THz		
Visible Light	400 THz – 700 THz	400 nm – 700 nm	Moderate
Ultraviolet (UV)	700 THz – 30 PHz	10 nm – 400 nm	High
X-Rays	30 PHz – 30 EHz	0.01 nm – 10 nm	Very High
Gamma Rays	> 30 EHz	< 0.01 nm	Extremely High

(GHz: Gigahertz, THz: Terahertz, PHz: Petahertz, EHz: Exahertz, nm: nanometers, m: meters)

2. Types of Electromagnetic Radiation

2.1 Radio Waves

- **Wavelength:** > 1 m
- **Frequency:** < 3 GHz
- **Energy Level:** Lowest
- **Uses:**
  - AM/FM Radio & TV Broadcasting
  - Mobile Communication (2G, 3G, 4G, 5G)
  - GPS & Wireless Communication
  - MRI (Medical Imaging)
- **Effects on Living Beings:**
  - Generally considered non-ionizing and safe at low intensities.
  - Prolonged exposure to high-intensity radio waves may cause thermal effects.

2.2 Microwaves

- **Wavelength:** 1 mm – 1 m
- **Frequency:** 3 GHz – 300 GHz
- **Uses:**
  - Microwave Ovens
  - Satellite & Mobile Communication
  - Radar Systems

- Wireless Networks (Wi-Fi, Bluetooth)
- **Effects on Living Beings:**
  - Can heat body tissues due to absorption (used in microwave ovens).
  - Potential risks with prolonged exposure to high-intensity microwaves.

2.3 Infrared (IR) Radiation

- **Wavelength:** 700 nm – 1 mm
- **Frequency:** 300 GHz – 400 THz
- **Uses:**
  - Remote Controls
  - Thermal Imaging & Night Vision
  - Heating Systems (Infrared Heaters)
  - Optical Fiber Communication
- **Effects on Living Beings:**
  - Excessive IR exposure can cause burns and eye damage.
  - Used in medical treatments (infrared therapy).

2.4 Visible Light

- **Wavelength:** 400 nm – 700 nm
- **Frequency:** 400 THz – 700 THz
- **Uses:**
  - Human Vision
  - Photosynthesis in Plants
  - Optical Communication (Lasers, Fiber Optics)
- **Effects on Living Beings:**
  - Essential for vision and biological functions.
  - Overexposure to intense light can cause eye strain or blindness.

2.5 Ultraviolet (UV) Radiation

- **Wavelength:** 10 nm – 400 nm
- **Frequency:** 700 THz – 30 PHz
- **Uses:**
  - Sterilization & Disinfection
  - Sunlight (Vitamin D Production)
  - Fluorescent Lighting
- **Effects on Living Beings:**
  - Can cause skin burns, premature aging, and skin cancer.
  - High doses can damage DNA and cause mutations.

2.6 X-Rays

- **Wavelength:** 0.01 nm – 10 nm
- **Frequency:** 30 PHz – 30 EHz
- **Uses:**
  - Medical Imaging (X-rays, CT Scans)
  - Security Screening (Airport Scanners)
  - Industrial Inspection
- **Effects on Living Beings:**
  - Can penetrate soft tissues and affect internal organs.
  - Excessive exposure leads to radiation poisoning and increased cancer risk.

2.7 Gamma Rays

- **Wavelength:** < 0.01 nm
- **Frequency:** > 30 EHz
- **Uses:**
  - Cancer Treatment (Radiotherapy)
  - Nuclear Reactions & Atomic Bombs
  - Space Exploration & Astronomy

- **Effects on Living Beings:**
  - Highly penetrating radiation that can damage DNA.
  - Prolonged exposure leads to severe health hazards, including radiation sickness and cancer.

3. Conclusion

Electromagnetic radiation plays a vital role in daily life, from communication and healthcare to industrial applications. However, understanding the effects of different types of EM waves is crucial to minimize risks and harness their benefits safely.

SOURCES OF ELECTROMAGNETIC RADIATION (NATURAL & MAN-MADE)

Electromagnetic (EM) radiation originates from **natural** and **man-made** sources. These sources emit different types of EM waves, ranging from low-energy radio waves to high-energy gamma rays. Understanding their origin helps in assessing their effects on living beings.

1. Natural Sources of Electromagnetic Radiation

Nature provides various sources of EM radiation, many of which are essential for life and planetary functions.

1.1 The Sun (Primary Source)

- The **Sun** is the most significant natural source of EM radiation.
- It emits a broad spectrum, including **radio waves, infrared, visible light, ultraviolet (UV), X-rays, and gamma rays**.
- Benefits:
  ○ Essential for **photosynthesis** in plants.
  ○ Provides **visible light** for vision.
  ○ Generates **UV radiation** for vitamin D

synthesis.

- Risks:
  - **UV radiation** can cause **sunburn, skin cancer, and eye damage.**
  - Solar flares release **X-rays and gamma rays,** which can impact satellites and power grids.

1.2 Cosmic Radiation (Space Sources)

- Cosmic rays and EM radiation from space originate from **stars, supernovae, black holes, and quasars.**
- **Gamma rays and X-rays** from distant galaxies and neutron stars are detected on Earth.
- Earth's **magnetic field and atmosphere** shield us from excessive exposure.
- High-altitude flights and astronauts are more exposed to cosmic radiation.

1.3 Lightning and Electrical Storms

- Lightning produces **radio waves, visible light, infrared radiation**, and even **X-rays and gamma rays.**
- **Terrestrial Gamma-ray Flashes (TGFs)** are bursts of gamma radiation produced during intense thunderstorms.
- **Effects:**
  - Can interfere with **radio communications.**
  - High-energy emissions can affect atmospheric chemistry.

1.4 The Earth's Own Radiation (Terrestrial Radiation)

- The Earth's **crust** emits low levels of **radio waves, infrared, and natural gamma radiation.**
- **Radon gas**, a radioactive element found in rocks, releases **alpha particles and gamma rays.**

- **Thermal infrared radiation** is emitted from the Earth's surface, contributing to the **greenhouse effect**.

1.5 The Human Body (Biological EM Radiation)

- The human body emits **infrared radiation (heat)** due to metabolic activity.
- The brain and nervous system generate **low-frequency electrical signals**, which can be detected using EEG machines.
- Some studies suggest **biophotons** (very weak light emissions) may be present in cells.

2. Man-Made Sources of Electromagnetic Radiation

With technological advancements, humans have developed artificial sources of EM radiation, ranging from communication devices to industrial applications.

2.1 Power Lines & Electrical Appliances

- Power lines emit **low-frequency (ELF) electromagnetic fields** (50-60 Hz).
- Household appliances (microwaves, refrigerators, televisions) generate **radio waves and infrared radiation.**
- **Effects:**
    - Generally safe, but prolonged exposure to high-voltage power lines is a subject of study for potential health risks.

2.2 Radio & TV Transmitters

- AM/FM radio, television, and satellite communications rely on **radio waves and microwaves.**
- **Effects:**
    - Can cause **electromagnetic interference (EMI)** with nearby devices.

◦ High exposure (e.g., workers near powerful transmitters) may experience **thermal effects**.

2.3 Mobile Phones & Wireless Communication (Wi-Fi, Bluetooth, 5G)

- **Mobile networks** (2G, 3G, 4G, 5G) emit **radiofrequency (RF) radiation**.
- **Wi-Fi routers** and **Bluetooth devices** use microwave frequencies.
- **Effects:**
  ◦ Non-ionizing radiation, but concerns exist over long-term exposure.
  ◦ Ongoing research explores potential links to sleep disturbances, headaches, and cognitive effects.

2.4 Medical Imaging & Radiation Therapy

- **X-ray machines** and **CT scans** use **X-rays** for diagnostic imaging.
- **MRI (Magnetic Resonance Imaging)** uses **radio waves and strong magnetic fields**.
- **Radiotherapy (Cancer Treatment)** uses high-energy **X-rays or gamma rays** to destroy cancer cells.
- **Effects:**
  ◦ Beneficial in controlled medical use.
  ◦ Prolonged or excessive exposure increases **radiation damage risk**.

2.5 Nuclear Power Plants & Weapons

- **Nuclear reactors** emit **gamma rays** as part of controlled nuclear reactions.
- **Nuclear weapons** release intense **gamma radiation** and **ionizing radiation** during explosions.

- **Effects:**
  - Controlled radiation in power plants is managed to minimize exposure.
  - Nuclear accidents (e.g., Chernobyl, Fukushima) expose people to harmful levels of radiation, leading to genetic mutations and cancer.

2.6 Household & Industrial Sources

- **Microwave ovens** emit microwaves to heat food.

- **Infrared heaters** and remote controls use **infrared (IR) radiation**.

- **LED lights, CFL bulbs, and lasers** emit **visible and UV light**.

- **Industrial welding** produces **UV, visible, and infrared radiation**.

- **Effects:**
  - Excessive exposure to certain sources (e.g., welding without protection) can lead to **burns, eye damage, and skin disorders**.

2.7 Satellites & Space Technology

- GPS satellites, communication satellites, and space probes transmit **radio and microwave signals**.

- The **International Space Station (ISS)** experiences **higher cosmic radiation levels** due to reduced atmospheric protection.

3. Comparison of Natural vs. Man-Made EM Radiation

Factor	Natural Sources	Man-Made Sources
Types of EM Waves	Radio, Infrared, Visible, UV, X-rays, Gamma	Radio, Microwaves, Infrared, UV, X-rays, Gamma

Primary Sources	Sun, Earth, Cosmic Rays, Lightning	Mobile Networks, Wi-Fi, Power Lines, Medical Devices
Energy Levels	Mostly moderate to high	Varies (low for Wi-Fi, high for X-ray machines)
Effects on Health	Essential (e.g., sunlight) but also harmful in excess (e.g., UV, cosmic rays)	Dependent on intensity, duration, and proximity
Control Measures	Limited (except for UV protection)	Regulatory limits for mobile radiation, medical imaging safety standards

4. Conclusion

Electromagnetic radiation is present everywhere, from natural cosmic rays to artificial mobile networks. While some forms are beneficial (e.g., visible light, radio waves for communication), others require careful management to prevent harmful effects (e.g., prolonged UV exposure, excessive X-rays).

SPECTRUM CLASSIFICATION: RADIO WAVES TO GAMMA RAYS

The **electromagnetic (EM) spectrum** is the range of all types of electromagnetic radiation, classified based on **wavelength** and **frequency**. These waves vary in their energy levels and interactions with matter, influencing their applications and effects on living beings.

---

1. Overview of the Electromagnetic Spectrum

Electromagnetic waves are characterized by:

- **Wavelength (λ)**: Distance between two wave peaks (measured in meters).

- **Frequency (v)**: Number of wave cycles per second (measured in Hertz, Hz).

- **Energy (E)**: Related to frequency, measured in electron volts (eV).

The **relationship between these properties** is governed by the equation:

$$c = \lambda v$$

where:

- c = Speed of light (3.0×10^8 m/s)
- λ = Wavelength (m)
- ν = Frequency (Hz)

Energy of a photon is given by:

$$E = h\nu$$

where:

- h = Planck's constant (6.626×10^{-34} J·s)

2. Electromagnetic Spectrum Categories

The EM spectrum is divided into different categories, arranged from **longest wavelength & lowest energy** (radio waves) to **shortest wavelength & highest energy** (gamma rays).

2.1 Radio Waves (30 Hz – 300 GHz, λ > 1 mm)

- **Wavelength Range**: 1 mm to 100 km
- **Frequency Range**: 30 Hz to 300 GHz
- **Energy**: $<10^{-5}$ eV (Lowest)
- **Uses:**
  - AM/FM radio broadcasting
  - Television signals
  - Mobile communication (2G, 3G, 4G, 5G)
  - GPS systems
- **Effects on Living Beings:**
  - Non-ionizing; does not damage DNA.
  - Prolonged exposure to strong radio waves (e.g., near high-power transmitters) may cause slight **heating effects**.

2.2 Microwaves (300 MHz – 300 GHz, λ = 1 mm to 1 m)

- **Wavelength Range**: 1 mm to 1 m
- **Frequency Range**: 300 MHz to 300 GHz

- **Energy**: $10^{-5} - 10^{-3}$ eV
- **Uses**:
    - Microwave ovens (2.45 GHz)
    - Satellite & space communications
    - Radar & weather monitoring
    - Wi-Fi (2.4 GHz, 5 GHz, 6 GHz)
- **Effects on Living Beings**:
    - Non-ionizing but causes **thermal effects** (heating of water molecules in tissues).
    - Excessive exposure may lead to **burns or cataracts**.

2.3 Infrared (IR) Radiation (300 GHz – 400 THz, λ = 700 nm to 1 mm)

- **Wavelength Range**: 700 nm to 1 mm
- **Frequency Range**: 300 GHz to 400 THz
- **Energy**: 10^{-3} - 1 eV
- **Uses**:
    - Night vision devices & thermal imaging
    - Remote controls
    - Infrared heaters
    - Medical imaging & physiotherapy
- **Effects on Living Beings**:
    - **Mild heating effects**; prolonged exposure can lead to **skin burns**.
    - Infrared lasers may cause **eye damage**.

2.4 Visible Light (400 – 700 THz, λ = 380 – 700 nm)

- **Wavelength Range**: 380 nm to 700 nm
- **Frequency Range**: 400 THz to 700 THz
- **Energy**: 1 - 3 eV

- **Uses:**
    - Human vision (sunlight, artificial lighting)
    - Photosynthesis in plants
    - Optical fiber communication
    - Laser applications
- **Effects on Living Beings:**
    - Essential for life but excessive exposure (e.g., bright sunlight) can cause **eye strain and damage**.
    - Blue light from screens may affect **sleep cycles** (circadian rhythms).

2.5 Ultraviolet (UV) Radiation (10^{15} – 10^{17} Hz, λ = 10 – 400 nm)

- **Wavelength Range:** 10 nm to 400 nm

- **Frequency Range:** 10^{15}–10^{17} Hz

- **Energy:** 3 - 124 eV

- **Types of UV Radiation:**
    - **UV-A (315-400 nm):** Least harmful; penetrates deeper into skin.
    - **UV-B (280-315 nm):** Causes sunburn; linked to skin cancer.
    - **UV-C (100-280 nm):** Most harmful, but mostly absorbed by Earth's ozone layer.

- **Uses:**
    - Sterilization & disinfection (UV-C lamps)
    - Tanning beds
    - Fluorescent lamps

- **Effects on Living Beings:**
    - Causes **DNA damage**, leading to **mutations, aging, and skin cancer**.
    - Can **harm the eyes** (photokeratitis, cataracts).

2.6 X-Rays (10^{17} – 10^{19} Hz, λ = 0.01 – 10 nm)

- **Wavelength Range**: 0.01 nm to 10 nm

- **Frequency Range**: $10^{17} - 10^{19}$ Hz

- **Energy**: 124 eV - 100 keV

- **Uses**:
  - Medical imaging (X-ray scans, CT scans)
  - Airport security screening
  - Industrial non-destructive testing

- **Effects on Living Beings**:
  - **Ionizing radiation**: Can **damage DNA** and cause **cancer**.
  - High doses can lead to **radiation sickness**.

2.7 Gamma Rays (10^{19} – 10^{24} Hz, λ < 0.01 nm)

- **Wavelength Range**: < 0.01 nm

- **Frequency Range**: $10^{19} - 10^{24}$ Hz

- **Energy**: 100 keV - 10 MeV (Highest)

- **Sources**:
  - Radioactive decay (e.g., Uranium, Cobalt-60)
  - Cosmic rays & supernovae
  - Nuclear explosions

- **Uses**:
  - Cancer radiotherapy
  - Sterilization of food & medical equipment
  - Space research

- **Effects on Living Beings**:
  - **Highly penetrative and ionizing.**
  - Causes **severe DNA damage, mutations, radiation poisoning**.
  - Can lead to **acute radiation sickness and death** in extreme exposures.

3. Summary of the Electromagnetic Spectrum

Radiation Type	Wavelength	Frequency	Energy	Effects on Living Beings
Radio Waves	>1 mm	<300 GHz	$<10^{-5}$ eV	Non-ionizing, minimal effects
Microwaves	1 mm – 1 m	300 MHz – 300 GHz	10^{-5}–10^{-3} eV	Can cause heating effects
Infrared (IR)	700 nm – 1 mm	300 GHz – 400 THz	10^{-3} - 1 eV	Mild heating, eye damage
Visible Light	380 – 700 nm	400 – 700 THz	1 - 3 eV	Essential for vision, excess can damage eyes
Ultraviolet (UV)	10 – 400 nm	10^{15}–10^{17} Hz	3 - 124 eV	DNA damage, skin cancer
X-Rays	0.01 – 10 nm	10^{17}–10^{19} Hz	124 eV - 100 keV	Ionizing, can cause cancer
Gamma Rays	< 0.01 nm	10^{19}–10^{24} Hz	100 keV - 10 MeV	Highly dangerous, radiation sickness

BIOLOGICAL EFFECTS OF ELECTROMAGNETIC RADIATION

The biological impact of electromagnetic (EM) radiation on living beings depends on **wavelength, frequency, energy, and exposure duration**. EM waves are classified into **non-ionizing radiation** (low energy) and **ionizing radiation** (high energy), with different effects on biological tissues.

1. Non-Ionizing Radiation Effects

(Does not have enough energy to remove electrons from atoms but can cause heating or other indirect biological effects.)

1.1 Radio Waves (30 Hz – 300 GHz)

- **Effects on Humans & Animals:**
  - Generally considered safe at normal exposure levels.
  - Prolonged exposure to high-intensity radio waves (near transmission towers or industrial sources) may cause:
    - **Mild tissue heating**.
    - **Headaches or dizziness** (subjective effects).
    - **Electromagnetic   Hypersensitivity**

(EHS) (though not scientifically proven).

- Studies on mobile phone radiation (700 MHz – 3 GHz) suggest possible links to **long-term neurological effects**, but no conclusive evidence of cancer risk.

. **Effects on Plants & Environment:**

- Some studies suggest changes in **plant growth** near radio transmitters.

- Disrupts **bird navigation** due to interference with Earth's natural electromagnetic fields.

1.2 Microwaves (300 MHz – 300 GHz)

. **Effects on Humans & Animals:**

- Can penetrate tissues and cause **thermal effects** (heating of body tissues).

- **Prolonged exposure** (e.g., industrial microwave radiation leaks) may cause:
  - **Cataracts** (due to heating of eye tissues).
  - **Nerve damage** with long exposure at high power.

- **Mobile Phones (2G, 3G, 4G, 5G):**
  - No clear evidence of cancer risk, but **long-term exposure is still under study.**
  - Some studies suggest a **slight increase in brain tumor risk** with heavy phone usage (>10 years).

. **Effects on Plants & Environment:**

- Studies suggest possible effects on **seed germination and plant growth.**

- Some reports indicate microwave radiation affects **insect populations (e.g., bees, butterflies)** by altering navigation behavior.

1.3 Infrared (IR) Radiation (700 nm – 1 mm)

- **Effects on Humans & Animals:**
  - **Mild exposure**: Generates warmth and aids **blood circulation** (used in heat therapy).
  - **Prolonged exposure:**
    - Skin burns and **heat-induced stress.**
    - Eye damage (**retinal burns**, cataracts).
  - **Infrared lasers** can cause **permanent tissue damage.**
- **Effects on Plants & Environment:**
  - **Excess IR exposure** can alter **photosynthesis rates.**
  - Can lead to **water loss in plants**, affecting growth.

1.4 Visible Light (380 – 700 nm)

- **Effects on Humans & Animals:**
  - Essential for **vision and circadian rhythms.**
  - **Overexposure to blue light (from screens, LEDs)** may:
    - Disrupt sleep cycles.
    - Increase risk of **macular degeneration** (long-term eye damage).
  - **Intense light (e.g., lasers, welding arcs)** can cause:
    - **Eye burns and blindness** (retinal damage).
    - **Skin irritation** at high intensities.
- **Effects on Plants & Environment:**
  - **Crucial for photosynthesis.**
  - Artificial light pollution can disrupt **nocturnal wildlife** (e.g., insects, migratory birds).

1.5 Ultraviolet (UV) Radiation (10 – 400 nm)

- **Effects on Humans & Animals:**
  - UV radiation is divided into:

- **UV-A (315-400 nm)**: Causes skin aging, DNA mutations.
- **UV-B (280-315 nm)**: Causes sunburn, DNA damage, skin cancer.
- **UV-C (100-280 nm)**: Most harmful but absorbed by ozone.
  - **Short-term effects**:
    - **Sunburn, photokeratitis (snow blindness), DNA damage**.
  - **Long-term effects**:
    - Increased risk of **skin cancer (melanoma, carcinoma)**.
    - **Premature aging** of skin.
    - Increased risk of **cataracts and eye damage**.

- **Effects on Plants & Environment:**
  - UV-B affects **plant metabolism and photosynthesis**.
  - Can damage **phytoplankton**, disrupting marine ecosystems.
  - UV-C is used in **sterilization** (destroys microbes).

2. Ionizing Radiation Effects

(High-energy radiation that can **ionize atoms and break chemical bonds**, leading to severe biological damage.)

2.1 X-Rays (0.01 – 10 nm)

- **Effects on Humans & Animals:**
  - **Short-term exposure**:
    - Used in medical imaging (safe at low doses).
    - Excessive exposure can cause **radiation burns**.
  - **Long-term exposure**:
    - Can cause **mutations, cancer, and DNA**

damage.

- Occupational exposure (e.g., radiologists) needs **protective shielding**.

. **Effects on Plants & Environment:**
  ◦ Can cause **genetic mutations in plants**.
  ◦ High doses reduce plant growth and affect **crop yields**.

2.2 Gamma Rays (< 0.01 nm)

. **Effects on Humans & Animals:**
  ◦ Highly **penetrating and dangerous**.
  ◦ **Acute exposure (e.g., nuclear radiation):**
    - Causes **radiation sickness** (nausea, burns, organ failure).
    - **High doses (above 5 Sv) are fatal.**
  ◦ **Long-term exposure:**
    - Causes **DNA mutations, cancer, and birth defects**.
    - Affects bone marrow, leading to **leukemia**.

. **Effects on Plants & Environment:**
  ◦ High doses lead to **stunted plant growth, mutations**.
  ◦ Can cause **genetic alterations in animals**.
  ◦ **Nuclear disasters (Chernobyl, Fukushima)** caused **widespread ecosystem damage**.

3. Summary of Biological Effects

Radiation Type	Short-Term Effects	Long-Term Effects	Effects on Plants & Environment
Radio Waves	No direct effects	Possible mild thermal effects	Possible effects on bird navigation
Microwaves	Tissue heating, eye damage	Possible neurological effects	May affect seed germination, insects
Infrared	Skin burns, eye damage	Possible tissue damage	Can alter plant metabolism

Visible Light	Eye strain, sleep disruption	Risk of retinal damage	Crucial for photosynthesis
Ultraviolet (UV)	Sunburn, DNA damage	Skin cancer, aging, cataracts	Affects phytoplankton, plant growth
X-Rays	Radiation burns	Cancer, genetic mutations	Reduces plant growth
Gamma Rays	Radiation sickness, organ failure	Cancer, genetic damage	Environmental contamination, mutations

4. Protection Against EM Radiation

- **Shielding**: Lead shields (X-rays, gamma rays), Faraday cages (radio waves).

- **Minimizing Exposure**: Limited mobile phone use, avoiding prolonged UV exposure.

- **Protective Gear**: Sunglasses (UV), radiation suits (gamma rays).

- **Regulations & Standards**: Organizations like WHO, ICRP, and FCC set exposure limits.

BASICS OF ELECTROMAGNETIC WAVE PROPAGATION

Electromagnetic (EM) waves are **self-propagating transverse waves** consisting of **electric (E) and magnetic (B) fields** oscillating perpendicular to each other and to the direction of wave travel. They move through space at the speed of light (**c ≈ 3 × 10^8 m/s in a vacuum**) and do not require a medium for propagation.

1. Properties of Electromagnetic Waves

- **Transverse Nature:** The electric field (**E**) and magnetic field (**B**) are perpendicular to each other and the direction of propagation.

- **Self-Sustaining:** The oscillating electric field generates a magnetic field, and vice versa.

- **Speed of Propagation:**
  - In vacuum: $c = 3 \times 10^8$ m/s
  - In a medium: $v = c/n$, where n is the refractive index of the medium.

- **Wavelength & Frequency Relationship:**
  - $c = \lambda f$ f, where:
    - c = speed of light
    - λ = wavelength
    - f = frequency

- **Energy & Frequency Relation**:
    - Energy of a photon: E=hf (where h is Planck's constant).

---

2. Modes of Electromagnetic Wave Propagation

2.1 Free Space Propagation

- EM waves travel through vacuum or air **without needing a medium**.
- Example: Light from the Sun reaching Earth.

2.2 Ground Wave Propagation (Surface Waves)

- Waves travel along Earth's surface.
- Used for **low-frequency radio waves (AM radio, maritime communication)**.
- **Limited by Earth's curvature** (maximum range: ~1000 km).

2.3 Skywave Propagation (Ionospheric Reflection)

- **High-frequency (HF) radio waves (3-30 MHz)** reflect off the **ionosphere**, allowing long-distance communication.
- Used in **shortwave radio, amateur radio, military communication**.
- Affected by **solar activity and atmospheric conditions**.

2.4 Space Wave Propagation (Line-of-Sight Transmission)

- Used in **microwave, VHF/UHF radio, TV broadcasts, satellite communication**.
- Requires **direct visibility** between transmitter and receiver.
- Limited by Earth's curvature (except in satellites).

2.5 Waveguides & Fiber Optics

- **Guided propagation** of EM waves through cables,

optical fibers.

- **Fiber optics** use total internal reflection to transmit light over long distances with minimal loss.

3. Factors Affecting EM Wave Propagation

3.1 Medium Properties

- **Permittivity (ε)**: Determines how an electric field interacts with the medium.
- **Permeability (μ)**: Determines how a magnetic field interacts with the medium.
- **Conductivity (σ)**: Conductive materials absorb EM waves (used in shielding).

3.2 Atmospheric Effects

- **Absorption**: Water vapor and gases absorb certain frequencies (e.g., **microwaves absorbed by water molecules**).
- **Scattering**: Shorter wavelengths (blue light) scatter more than longer wavelengths (red light) → **reason for blue sky**.
- **Refraction**: EM waves bend when passing through different media (used in optical lenses, mirages).
- **Ionospheric Reflection**: Affects HF radio signals.

3.3 Obstacles & Diffraction

- **Diffraction**: EM waves bend around obstacles, allowing reception beyond line of sight.
- **Multipath Fading**: Signals take multiple paths due to reflection, causing interference.

4. Applications of EM Wave Propagation

- **Communication**: Radio, TV, mobile networks, satellites.

- **Navigation**: GPS, radar systems.
- **Medical Imaging**: X-rays, MRI.
- **Remote Sensing**: Weather forecasting, military surveillance.

MECHANISMS OF ELECTROMAGNETIC (EM) INTERACTION WITH LIVING CELLS

Electromagnetic (EM) waves interact with biological systems in complex ways, depending on their frequency, intensity, duration of exposure, and biological characteristics of the cells. The interaction can be classified into **thermal**, **non-thermal**, and **ionizing effects**, impacting cellular structures and physiological processes.

1. Types of EM Interactions with Living Cells

1.1 Thermal Effects (Heating of Tissue)

- **Mechanism**: High-frequency EM waves (e.g., microwaves, radio waves) cause molecular vibrations, leading to heat generation in tissues.

- **Examples**:
  - Microwave ovens heat food via dielectric heating.
  - Mobile phones and Wi-Fi signals cause mild tissue warming.
  - MRI scanners use radio waves, but controlled for medical imaging.

- **Biological Impact**:
  - Excessive heating can cause **protein**

denaturation, cell membrane damage, and **burn injuries**.

- The **Specific Absorption Rate (SAR)** measures the rate of EM energy absorption in human tissue (higher SAR = more heating).
- Long-term exposure might impact **brain function, fertility, and skin health**.

1.2 Non-Thermal Effects (Subtle Cellular Disruptions)

- **Mechanism:**
  - EM fields interact with cell membranes, proteins, and DNA without significant heating.
  - Can alter **ion channel activity, neurotransmitter release, and genetic expression**.

- **Examples:**
  - **Low-frequency EM fields** (e.g., power lines, electrical appliances) may affect **nervous system function**.
  - **Radiofrequency (RF) exposure** is linked to **oxidative stress** in cells, potentially causing **DNA damage**.
  - Some studies suggest **changes in melatonin production**, impacting sleep cycles.

- **Biological Impact:**
  - Altered **hormone levels, disrupted cell communication**, and **potential long-term neurological effects**.
  - Some reports indicate possible effects on **memory, focus, and learning**.

1.3 Ionizing Effects (DNA Damage & Cellular Mutations)

- **Mechanism:**
  - High-energy EM waves (e.g., X-rays, gamma rays) have enough energy to ionize atoms,

breaking chemical bonds in biological molecules.

- Direct damage to **DNA strands**, causing **mutations, chromosomal aberrations, and cancer risks**.

- **Examples**:
  - **UV radiation** from the Sun can cause **skin cancer** (UV-induced DNA mutations).
  - **X-rays & gamma rays** are used in **radiotherapy** to kill cancer cells but can also damage healthy tissues.
  - **Nuclear radiation exposure** can cause **cell apoptosis (cell death) and genetic disorders**.

- **Biological Impact**:
  - Increased risk of **cancer, radiation sickness, genetic mutations**.
  - **Acute radiation syndrome (ARS)** in high-exposure cases.
  - Controlled exposure is used in **medical imaging & cancer treatments**.

2. Key Biological Targets Affected by EM Waves

2.1 Cell Membrane

- **Altered permeability**: EM fields can change the way ions and molecules pass through membranes, affecting cell communication.

- **Protein & lipid disruption**: Changes in membrane proteins can lead to altered cellular functions.

2.2 DNA & Genetic Material

- **DNA strand breaks**: Ionizing radiation (X-rays, gamma rays) can cause **double-strand DNA breaks**, leading to mutations.

- **Epigenetic changes**: Some EM fields may affect gene expression without altering DNA sequences.

2.3 Nervous System & Brain Function

- **Neuronal signaling disruption**: EM exposure can influence **neurotransmitter release**, impacting sleep, mood, and cognition.
- **Blood-brain barrier effects**: Some studies suggest **prolonged mobile phone radiation** may weaken the **brain's protective barrier**, increasing toxin entry.

2.4 Immune System Response

- Some research indicates **long-term EM exposure** may suppress immune responses, making individuals more vulnerable to diseases.

3. Adaptive Responses & Repair Mechanisms

- **DNA repair systems**: Cells can naturally repair some radiation-induced DNA damage.
- **Heat-shock proteins (HSPs)**: Cells produce HSPs to counteract thermal stress from EM exposure.
- **Melatonin production**: Acts as an antioxidant, potentially reducing EM-induced oxidative stress.

4. Potential Health Risks & Controversies

- **Cancer Risk:**
  - WHO classifies RF radiation as a **possible carcinogen** (Group 2B).
  - Mixed results on whether **mobile phone usage** increases brain tumor risk.
- **Electromagnetic Hypersensitivity (EHS):**
  - Some individuals report symptoms (headache, fatigue, dizziness) due to EM exposure, but scientific evidence remains inconclusive.
- **Fertility Concerns:**
  - Studies suggest **RF exposure** may reduce **sperm quality** and **egg viability**.

5. Mitigation Strategies & Safety Guidelines

- **Limit exposure**: Reduce excessive use of mobile phones, Wi-Fi, and prolonged screen time.

- **Use shielding devices**: EM shielding materials (Faraday cages) can reduce exposure.

- **Follow regulatory guidelines**: Governments set **SAR limits** for safe mobile phone radiation levels.

- **Medical monitoring**: Routine checkups for professionals exposed to high EM radiation (e.g., radiologists, power plant workers).

Conclusion

Electromagnetic waves interact with living cells in multiple ways, from harmless interactions to potential health risks. While **thermal and ionizing effects** are well understood, **non-thermal biological effects remain a topic of ongoing research**. Safe usage of EM-emitting devices and adherence to exposure guidelines can help mitigate risks while benefiting from technological advancements.

ABSORPTION, REFLECTION, AND PENETRATION OF ELECTROMAGNETIC (EM) WAVES

When electromagnetic (EM) waves interact with a material or biological system, they can undergo **absorption, reflection, or penetration (transmission).** These interactions depend on the **frequency of the wave, the properties of the material, and environmental factors.** Understanding these mechanisms is crucial in fields such as **medicine, telecommunications, defense, and biological research.**

1. Absorption of EM Waves

What is Absorption?

Absorption occurs when an EM wave's energy is taken in by a material, leading to **heating, molecular excitation, or electronic transitions.** The absorbed energy may then be converted into **heat, chemical changes, or electrical signals** in biological systems.

Factors Affecting Absorption:

- **Frequency & Wavelength:**
    - **Radio waves** pass through the body with

minimal absorption.

- **Microwaves** can cause tissue heating (used in microwave ovens and RF therapies).
- **Infrared waves** are absorbed by water molecules, producing heat.
- **Visible light & UV rays** are absorbed by pigments (e.g., melanin absorbs UV, causing skin tanning or burns).
- **X-rays & Gamma rays** penetrate tissues but are absorbed more by bones.

- **Material Composition:**
    - Water, fats, and proteins absorb EM waves differently.
    - Metal surfaces strongly absorb certain frequencies and convert them into heat.

- **Tissue Properties in Living Beings:**
    - Different body tissues absorb EM radiation at different rates.
    - **High-water-content tissues (e.g., muscles, eyes, brain)** absorb more energy than dry tissues (e.g., bones).

Biological Effects of EM Absorption:

- **Heat generation** in tissues (basis of RF and microwave therapies).
- **Altered cellular processes** due to non-thermal energy absorption.
- **Potential DNA damage** (if the energy is high enough, such as UV or X-rays).

Applications of Absorption:

- **Medical Imaging:** X-ray absorption in bones enables clear imaging.
- **Thermal Therapy:** Infrared and microwave treatments for muscle relaxation.

. **Energy Harvesting:** Solar cells absorb EM waves to generate electricity.

2. Reflection of EM Waves

What is Reflection?

Reflection occurs when an EM wave encounters a surface and **bounces back** instead of penetrating the material. The angle of incidence equals the angle of reflection (Law of Reflection).

Factors Affecting Reflection:

. **Surface Properties:**
  ◦ Smooth surfaces (like mirrors, polished metals) reflect EM waves in a single direction.
  ◦ Rough surfaces scatter waves in multiple directions.

. **Material Conductivity:**
  ◦ **Metals** reflect most EM waves due to free electrons (used in shielding).
  ◦ **Dielectric materials** (glass, plastics) allow some transmission and reflection.

. **Frequency & Wavelength:**
  ◦ Longer wavelengths (radio waves) can reflect off large objects.
  ◦ Shorter wavelengths (X-rays) penetrate deeply and reflect only at specific angles.

Biological Effects of Reflection:

. **Reduced EM exposure** behind reflective barriers (Faraday cages, shielding materials).

. **Interference patterns** from multiple reflections can impact **cellular signals and Wi-Fi** performance.

. **Skin reflection of visible light & UV** influences **tanning, burns, and vitamin D synthesis**.

Applications of Reflection:

. **Medical Imaging:** Ultrasound imaging relies on wave

reflection from tissues.

- **Radar Systems:** Aircraft and weather radars use radio wave reflection.
- **EM Shielding:** Reflective coatings protect sensitive electronics from interference.

3. Penetration (Transmission) of EM Waves

What is Penetration?

Penetration (or transmission) occurs when an EM wave **passes through a material** without being fully absorbed or reflected. The ability of a wave to penetrate depends on its **wavelength, frequency, and the properties of the medium**.

Factors Affecting Penetration:

- **Frequency & Wavelength:**
    - **Longer wavelengths (radio & microwaves)** penetrate deeper into biological tissues.
    - **Shorter wavelengths (UV, X-rays, gamma rays)** penetrate less but are more energetic.
- **Material Density:**
    - **Dense materials (bones, metals)** block EM waves.
    - **Less dense materials (skin, soft tissues, air)** allow penetration.
- **Moisture Content:**
    - Water-rich tissues absorb more energy, limiting penetration.
    - Dry environments allow better RF transmission.

Biological Effects of EM Penetration:

- **X-rays & Gamma Rays:** Deep penetration can cause **DNA damage and cancer risks**.
- **RF & Microwaves:** Can reach **internal organs, causing thermal effects**.

- **Visible & Infrared Light:** Can pass through the skin and affect underlying tissues.

Applications of Penetration:

- **Medical Imaging:**
  - X-rays pass through soft tissues but are absorbed by bones.
  - MRI uses RF waves for deep tissue imaging.

- **Wireless Communication:**
  - Radio waves penetrate walls and travel long distances.
  - 5G networks use high-frequency waves with limited penetration.

- **Food Processing:**
  - Microwaves penetrate food to heat it from within.

Comparison of Absorption, Reflection, and Penetration

Property	Absorption	Reflection	Penetration
Energy Transfer	Converted into heat/chemical energy	Bounced off the surface	Passed through the material
Effect on EM Wave	Wave loses energy & fades	Wave changes direction	Wave continues traveling
Depends on	Material properties, frequency	Surface smoothness, conductivity	Wavelength, density of material
Examples	X-ray absorption in bones, UV absorption in skin	Radar reflection, metallic shielding	Radio waves passing through walls, MRI scans

Conclusion

The interaction of EM waves with materials, including living tissues, involves absorption, reflection, and penetration. These mechanisms have **critical implications for health, communication, medical treatments, and engineering applications**. Proper understanding helps in designing **safer technologies, efficient medical devices, and protective measures against harmful EM exposure.**

THERMAL VS. NON-THERMAL EFFECTS OF ELECTROMAGNETIC (EM) RADIATION

Electromagnetic (EM) radiation interacts with biological tissues in two primary ways: **thermal effects** and **non-thermal effects**. These effects depend on the frequency, intensity, and duration of exposure to EM waves.

1. Thermal Effects of EM Radiation

Definition:

Thermal effects occur when **EM radiation increases the temperature of biological tissues** due to energy absorption. This is mainly observed in **radiofrequency (RF), microwave, and infrared (IR) radiation**, where absorbed energy leads to **heating effects** in tissues.

Mechanism of Thermal Effects:

- **EM waves transfer energy to biological tissues**, causing molecular vibrations.
- **Water molecules absorb energy and generate heat**, leading to tissue temperature rise.
- Excessive heating can lead to **cell damage, burns, or protein denaturation**.

Examples of Thermal Effects:

- **Microwave ovens** heat food by exciting water molecules.
- **Mobile phones & 5G networks** generate localized heating in tissues.
- **Infrared therapy** warms muscles and promotes blood circulation.
- **Prolonged laptop use** on the lap can increase skin temperature.
- **RF and microwave radiation exposure** in industrial settings may cause excessive heating in workers.

Biological Impact of Thermal Effects:

- **Mild heating (0.1–1°C):** Increased blood flow, cellular stimulation.
- **Moderate heating (1–3°C):** Temporary discomfort, tissue stress.
- **Severe heating (>3°C):** Burns, protein denaturation, irreversible cell damage.

Safety Standards & Limits:

Regulatory bodies like the **FCC (USA), ICNIRP (International), and WHO** set **specific absorption rate (SAR) limits** to prevent excessive thermal effects from devices like mobile phones.

---

2. Non-Thermal Effects of EM Radiation

Definition:

Non-thermal effects occur **without a significant increase in temperature**. These effects are observed at **low-intensity exposure** and are associated with **biological and neurological changes** rather than heating.

Mechanism of Non-Thermal Effects:

- EM fields can **alter cellular communication and**

signaling pathways.

- Changes in **ion channel activity, membrane potential, and gene expression**.
- Possible **oxidative stress, DNA damage, or hormonal disruption**.

Examples of Non-Thermal Effects:

- **Sleep disturbances** from prolonged exposure to mobile phone radiation.
- **Changes in brain activity & cognitive functions** due to low-frequency EM fields.
- **Electromagnetic hypersensitivity (EHS)**—a controversial condition where people report headaches, fatigue, and skin irritation from EM exposure.
- **Increased oxidative stress** leading to potential long-term health risks.

Biological Impact of Non-Thermal Effects:

- **Neurological:** Possible links to stress, anxiety, and cognitive changes.
- **Cellular:** Some studies suggest EM waves **affect DNA integrity**, though conclusive evidence is lacking.
- **Endocrine:** Possible influence on **melatonin and serotonin production**, affecting sleep cycles.
- **Immune System:** Potential modulation of immune responses in prolonged exposure scenarios.

Comparison: Thermal vs. Non-Thermal Effects

Feature	Thermal Effects	Non-Thermal Effects
Cause	Energy absorption leading to heating	Interaction with biological processes without heating

Frequency Range	RF, microwaves, infrared	Low-frequency EM waves, radio waves, UV, visible light
Primary Impact	Tissue heating, burns	Cellular, neurological, and hormonal effects
Examples	Microwave heating, mobile phone radiation	Sleep disturbance, oxidative stress, potential DNA damage
Regulation	SAR limits set by FCC, WHO, ICNIRP	Still under scientific debate, no strict limits in many cases

Conclusion:

While **thermal effects are well-established** and regulated, **non-thermal effects remain an area of ongoing research**. Some scientists argue that **long-term, low-intensity exposure** could have subtle but meaningful biological impacts.

BIOLOGICAL SAFETY MEASURES & EM SHIELDING TECHNIQUES

Exposure to electromagnetic (EM) radiation is an unavoidable part of modern life, given the widespread use of mobile phones, Wi-Fi, and electronic devices. While some levels of EM exposure are considered safe, long-term or high-intensity exposure may have biological effects. To mitigate potential risks, various **biological safety measures** and **EM shielding techniques** are used.

1. Biological Safety Measures

Biological safety measures aim to **reduce exposure to EM radiation** by modifying behaviors, regulating emissions, and designing safer environments.

A. Regulatory Exposure Limits

Governments and international bodies have established exposure limits to prevent excessive EM radiation exposure. These include:

- **SAR Limits**: The **Specific Absorption Rate (SAR)** is the amount of EM radiation absorbed by the human body.
  - Example: The **FCC** (USA) limits SAR for

mobile phones to **1.6 W/kg**, while **ICNIRP** (International Commission on Non-Ionizing Radiation Protection) sets the limit at **2.0 W/ kg**.

- **Power Density Limits**: The amount of EM energy in a given area, often regulated for **cell towers and industrial equipment**.

B. Reducing Exposure to EM Radiation

- **Limit Screen Time:** Reduce prolonged exposure to mobile phones and computers.

- **Use Speakerphones or Wired Headsets:** Decreases direct exposure from mobile phones.

- **Keep Distance from EM Sources:** Avoid placing devices like laptops directly on the body.

- **Turn Off Unused Devices:** Switching off Wi-Fi routers, Bluetooth, and electronic devices when not in use reduces unnecessary exposure.

- **Sleep Away from EM Sources:** Keep mobile phones and Wi-Fi routers away from sleeping areas to minimize night-time exposure.

C. Protective Wearables & Devices

- **Anti-Radiation Phone Cases:** Shield the body from excessive mobile radiation.

- **EMF-Blocking Clothing:** Special fabrics with metallic fibers can reduce exposure (e.g., silver-threaded fabric).

- **Radiation Shielding Stickers:** Marketed as EM absorbers, though their effectiveness is debated.

D. Smart Building Design

- **Low-Radiation Workspaces:** Offices with controlled Wi-Fi and EM exposure zones.

- **Shielded Walls & Windows:** Homes and workplaces

can integrate EM-blocking materials to reduce radiation penetration.

2. Electromagnetic Shielding Techniques

EM shielding prevents **unwanted EM waves** from interfering with sensitive electronics and human exposure.

A. Faraday Cage (Complete Shielding)

A **Faraday Cage** is an enclosure made of conductive materials (like copper or aluminum) that blocks EM fields.

- Used in **MRI rooms, laboratories, and military applications**.
- Protects electronic devices from **external EM interference**.

B. Shielding Materials

Specialized materials block or absorb EM waves:

- **Metal Foils (Copper, Aluminum, Silver):** Used in electronics and industrial shielding.
- **Conductive Paints:** Applied on walls to prevent RF radiation penetration.
- **EM-Blocking Fabrics:** Used in clothing, curtains, and workspaces.

C. Frequency-Specific Shielding

- **Low-Frequency (LF) Shielding:** Uses **ferrite cores** to block electrical fields from power cables.
- **High-Frequency (HF) Shielding:** Uses metal meshes, enclosures, and coatings to prevent radio and microwave radiation.

D. Shielding for Sensitive Areas

- **Hospitals & Research Labs:** MRI rooms are **completely shielded** to prevent interference.

- **Military & Government Facilities:** Secure rooms use Faraday shielding to prevent data theft.

- **Airplane Cockpits & Electronics:** Shielding prevents interference with navigation systems.

Conclusion

While EM radiation is a part of everyday life, **following safety measures** and **using shielding techniques** can help reduce potential biological effects.

SHORT-TERM EFFECTS OF ELECTROMAGNETIC (EM) RADIATION ON LIVING BEINGS

Short-term exposure to electromagnetic (EM) radiation can cause **immediate and temporary biological effects**, depending on the frequency, intensity, and duration of exposure. These effects can vary from **mild discomfort** to more **noticeable physiological changes**.

1. Common Short-Term Effects of EM Radiation

A. Thermal Effects (Heat-Related)

High-frequency EM waves (microwaves, radio waves) can **increase body temperature** by heating tissues.

- **Skin Heating & Burns:** Prolonged exposure to **high-intensity** EM waves can cause localized skin heating.
- **Eye Damage: Infrared radiation** or microwaves can heat the eye's lens, increasing the risk of **cataracts**.
- **Tissue Heating:** Prolonged use of mobile phones may cause a warming sensation around the ear.

B. Neurological Effects

Short-term exposure to EM radiation, especially from mobile phones and Wi-Fi routers, may affect brain activity.

- **Headaches & Dizziness:** Commonly reported after prolonged phone use.
- **Fatigue & Concentration Issues:** Weak EM fields may interfere with brain waves.
- **Sleep Disturbances:** Exposure to blue light and EM waves from screens at night **reduces melatonin production**, affecting sleep quality.

C. Cardiovascular Effects

- **Increased Heart Rate:** Studies suggest that short-term exposure to high-power EM fields may temporarily **increase heart rate** and **blood pressure**.
- **Blood Flow Changes:** Some research indicates **minor changes in blood circulation** due to prolonged RF exposure.

D. Muscle & Joint Discomfort

- **Tingling or Numbness:** Some individuals report a tingling sensation in fingers or hands after using **touchscreen devices for long periods**.
- **Muscle Fatigue:** Possible link between **low-frequency EM fields and temporary muscle weakness**.

E. Electromagnetic Hypersensitivity (EHS)

Some individuals claim to experience **heightened sensitivity to EM fields**, leading to symptoms like:

- **Skin irritation (redness, itching)**
- **Nausea and dizziness**
- **Eye strain and blurred vision**
- **Mental fog (difficulty thinking clearly)**

While **EHS is not officially recognized as a medical condition**, studies continue to explore its causes and effects.

2. Safety Tips to Reduce Short-Term Effects

- **Use Speakerphone or Headphones** instead of holding the phone directly to the ear.
- **Limit Screen Time Before Sleep** to avoid melatonin suppression.
- **Maintain Distance from EM Sources** (e.g., keep Wi-Fi routers away from bedrooms).
- **Take Breaks** from prolonged device use to avoid headaches and fatigue.
- **Use Anti-Radiation Shields** for mobile phones and laptops.

LONG-TERM EXPOSURE TO ELECTROMAGNETIC (EM) RADIATION AND HEALTH RISKS

Long-term exposure to electromagnetic (EM) radiation, particularly from sources such as mobile phones, Wi-Fi routers, power lines, and industrial equipment, has been a topic of extensive research. While regulatory bodies like the **WHO (World Health Organization)** and **ICNIRP (International Commission on Non-Ionizing Radiation Protection)** state that low-level EM exposure is generally safe, ongoing studies explore potential health risks.

1. Potential Long-Term Health Risks

A. Increased Risk of Cancer & Tumors

- Some studies suggest prolonged exposure to **radiofrequency (RF) radiation** from mobile phones **may be linked to brain tumors** like gliomas and acoustic neuromas.

- **IARC (International Agency for Research on Cancer)** classified RF radiation as **"possibly** carcinogenic" (Group 2B) based on limited human studies.

- Long-term **occupational exposure** to high-frequency EM waves (e.g., radar operators, telecom workers) has been examined for possible cancer risks.

B. Neurological & Cognitive Effects

- **Memory Loss & Cognitive Decline:** Long-term EM exposure has been associated with mild cognitive impairments, particularly in children and elderly individuals.

- **Increased Risk of Neurodegenerative Diseases:** Some studies suggest links between prolonged EM exposure and conditions like **Alzheimer's disease and Parkinson's disease**, though evidence is inconclusive.

- **Mental Health Issues:** Potential association with **anxiety, depression, and chronic stress** due to prolonged digital device use.

C. Cardiovascular Problems

- Long-term exposure to **low-frequency EM fields** (from power lines, household appliances) has been linked to **changes in heart rate and blood pressure**.

- Some studies indicate that prolonged exposure may increase the risk of **hypertension** and irregular heart rhythms.

D. Infertility & Reproductive Issues

- **Male Infertility:** Some research suggests **RF radiation from mobile phones** may reduce sperm quality, motility, and count.

- **Female Fertility & Pregnancy Risks:** Prolonged exposure to high EM fields may affect fetal development, although more research is needed.

E. DNA Damage & Oxidative Stress

- Long-term exposure may lead to **increased oxidative stress**, which can damage DNA and contribute to cell aging.

- **Free radicals** generated by prolonged EM exposure may lead to inflammatory conditions and chronic diseases.

F. Electromagnetic Hypersensitivity (EHS)

- Some individuals report long-term sensitivity to EM fields, leading to symptoms like **chronic fatigue, migraines, insomnia, and skin irritation**.

- While not officially classified as a medical condition, EHS remains an area of ongoing research.

2. Preventive Measures for Long-Term EM Exposure

A. Smart Device Usage

- **Limit Phone Calls & Use Wired Headsets** to reduce direct exposure.

- **Use Airplane Mode When Possible** to minimize unnecessary RF emissions.

- **Avoid Carrying Phones in Pockets** to reduce radiation exposure near vital organs.

B. Optimized Home & Workplace Environment

- **Keep Wi-Fi Routers Away from Sleeping Areas** to reduce nighttime exposure.

- **Use EM Shielding Materials** (e.g., Faraday cages, conductive paint, shielding fabrics).

- **Maintain Distance from High-EM Appliances** (microwaves, power lines, industrial equipment).

C. Government Regulations & Safety Standards

- **Adhering to ICNIRP & WHO Guidelines** for exposure limits.

- **Enforcing EMF shielding** in workplaces with high radiation levels.

- **Encouraging safer telecom infrastructure designs** to minimize radiation hotspots.

Conclusion

While definitive evidence on **long-term EM exposure risks** is still being researched, **precautionary measures** can help minimize potential health effects.

ELECTROMAGNETIC (EM) SIGNALS AND BRAIN FUNCTION

Electromagnetic (EM) radiation, particularly in the form of **radiofrequency (RF) radiation** emitted by devices like mobile phones, Wi-Fi routers, and microwaves, has raised concerns about its potential impact on **brain function** over prolonged exposure. Research on this topic is ongoing, and while some studies suggest minimal effects, others indicate that EM signals might influence **cognition, sleep**, and **stress**.

1. EM Signals and Cognition

Cognitive functions like memory, attention, decision-making, and learning can potentially be influenced by **EM exposure**, especially at high levels or over long durations.

A. Memory and Learning

- **Impaired Short-Term Memory:** Some studies suggest that long-term exposure to RF radiation could affect **short-term memory**. For example, studies conducted on individuals working in environments with high RF exposure (e.g., radio tower operators) found slight impairments in **verbal memory**.

- **Decreased Learning Capacity:** Animal studies have shown that continuous exposure to EM waves might alter the **brain's ability to process new information** or impair **spatial learning**, though results are mixed in human studies.

- **Neurotransmitter Imbalance:** EM radiation might affect the balance of neurotransmitters (chemicals that transmit signals between nerve cells), potentially impacting cognitive abilities.

B. Attention & Concentration

- **Difficulty Focusing:** Prolonged exposure to mobile phone radiation or continuous use of electronic devices could potentially **reduce the brain's ability to focus**. Some studies suggest that cognitive functions like attention span or multitasking abilities might be negatively affected.

- **Attention Deficits in Children:** Children may be more susceptible to cognitive disruptions due to developing brains. Some research has hinted at a possible connection between increased screen time and **attention problems** in children, but this remains an area of debate.

2. EM Signals and Sleep

Sleep patterns and quality may also be influenced by EM radiation, particularly from devices emitting **blue light** (smartphones, laptops) and RF radiation (mobile phones, Wi-Fi routers).

A. Sleep Disturbances

- **Disrupted Sleep Patterns: Exposure to EM fields** has been associated with **disruption of circadian rhythms**, leading to poorer sleep quality. For example, light emitted from screens (blue light) interferes with melatonin production, the hormone responsible for regulating sleep.

- **Delayed Sleep Onset:** People using devices like phones

or computers late at night might experience **delayed sleep onset**, meaning it takes longer to fall asleep, due to the suppression of melatonin production by blue light.

- **Insomnia: High-frequency RF exposure** from mobile phones or wireless devices could potentially lead to **sleep disturbances**, including trouble falling asleep and staying asleep. A few studies have shown that long-term exposure to EM radiation may **increase the risk of insomnia**.

- **Reduced Sleep Duration:** Continuous use of mobile phones, especially before bed, has been linked to **shortened sleep duration** in both adults and teenagers.

3. EM Signals and Stress

The relationship between EM signals and stress is complex, with research showing that prolonged exposure to EM radiation may induce **biological stress responses**.

A. Increased Cortisol Levels

- **Cortisol is a stress hormone** that regulates several bodily functions, including metabolism and immune response. Research indicates that exposure to **RF radiation** might lead to **increased cortisol levels**, which can elevate stress, disrupt metabolic processes, and impair immune function.

- **Heightened Stress Response:** Studies suggest that both **acute** and **chronic** exposure to EM radiation may **activate the body's stress response**, increasing the release of cortisol, which can result in feelings of anxiety and nervousness.

B. Increased Sympathetic Nervous System Activity

- **Fight-or-Flight Response:** Long-term exposure to EM

radiation might **stimulate the sympathetic nervous system**, which controls the **fight-or-flight response**. This could result in increased **heart rate, elevated blood pressure**, and **muscle tension**, contributing to stress and anxiety.

- **Chronic Stress:** Consistent exposure to EM radiation may contribute to **chronic stress**, potentially leading to long-term health problems like cardiovascular issues and mental health disorders (e.g., anxiety, depression).

4. Mechanisms of EM Radiation Affecting Brain Function

While the exact mechanisms are still under investigation, several theories attempt to explain how EM signals might impact the brain and its functions:

A. Electromagnetic Interference with Brain Activity

- **Electromagnetic fields** could potentially **interfere with electrical signals** in the brain, altering normal brain wave patterns. This interference could affect cognitive functions like concentration, memory, and decision-making.

- **Changes in Brainwave Patterns:** Some studies show changes in **brain wave patterns (alpha, beta, theta waves)** with prolonged exposure to EM radiation. These changes could disrupt the brain's ability to maintain focused or relaxed states, leading to cognitive and emotional difficulties.

B. Ion Channel Disruption

- **Ion channels** are proteins in cell membranes that regulate the flow of ions (charged particles) in and out of cells, which is crucial for **nerve signal transmission**. Some researchers propose that EM radiation could **disrupt ion channel functioning**, potentially affecting brain cells' ability to communicate effectively.

C. Oxidative Stress

- **Oxidative stress** occurs when there is an imbalance between free radicals (reactive oxygen species) and antioxidants in the body. EM radiation has been shown to increase oxidative stress in some cells, which can **damage brain cells** and contribute to neurological diseases, cognitive decline, and other health issues.

5. Preventive Measures

A. Minimize Screen Time

- **Limit exposure** to screens and devices that emit high-energy visible light (blue light) at least an hour before sleep to help maintain healthy circadian rhythms.
- **Use Blue Light Filters**: Apply blue light-blocking filters on screens or use **night mode** settings on devices to reduce blue light exposure.

B. EMF Shielding Techniques

- **Limit exposure** to EMF by keeping **distances from EM sources** like phones, Wi-Fi routers, and other devices emitting RF radiation.
- **Use EMF protection gear**, such as EMF-blocking phone cases, laptop shields, and other devices.

C. Mindfulness and Stress Reduction

- Engage in **relaxation techniques** (yoga, meditation, deep breathing) to mitigate stress caused by EM exposure.
- Regular **exercise** helps reduce the **negative impacts** of stress on both mental and physical health.

Conclusion

While the long-term effects of EM signals on brain function are still being researched, current evidence suggests that excessive or prolonged exposure may influence **cognition, sleep quality, and stress levels**. Understanding and managing EM exposure through **safety measures** and **smart device usage** can help minimize potential negative effects on brain health.

IMPACT OF ELECTROMAGNETIC (EM) SIGNALS ON THE NERVOUS SYSTEM

The **nervous system**, which includes the **central nervous system (CNS)** (brain and spinal cord) and the **peripheral nervous system (PNS)** (nerves outside the CNS), is highly sensitive to **electromagnetic (EM) radiation**. As the nervous system relies on electrical impulses to function, exposure to **external electromagnetic fields (EMFs)** can potentially interfere with normal neurological processes.

1. How EM Radiation Affects the Nervous System

A. Disruption of Neuronal Electrical Activity

- **Neurons** communicate through **electrical and chemical signals**. EM radiation, especially at high intensities, could potentially **interfere with nerve impulses**, leading to **neurological disturbances**.

- Some studies suggest that exposure to **radiofrequency (RF) radiation** from mobile phones, Wi-Fi, and power lines can **alter neuronal firing rates**, potentially affecting cognitive function and reflexes.

B. Alteration of Neurotransmitter Levels

- **Neurotransmitters** like **dopamine, serotonin, and acetylcholine** play critical roles in mood regulation, memory, and motor function.
- Some studies suggest that **chronic EM exposure** might lead to an imbalance in neurotransmitter levels, potentially contributing to **anxiety, depression, and cognitive dysfunction**.

C. Increased Oxidative Stress and Inflammation

- EM radiation has been shown to induce **oxidative stress** in the brain, leading to an accumulation of **reactive oxygen species (ROS)**.
- **Oxidative stress** can cause **neuroinflammation**, which is linked to neurological disorders like **Alzheimer's disease, Parkinson's disease, and multiple sclerosis (MS)**.
- Studies have found increased markers of **neural inflammation** in animals exposed to high EM radiation levels over extended periods.

2. Short-Term Effects on the Nervous System

A. Headaches and Dizziness

- Some individuals report experiencing **headaches, dizziness, or vertigo** after prolonged exposure to EM signals from mobile phones, Wi-Fi, or high-voltage power lines.
- While research remains inconclusive, **RF radiation exposure** may cause **temporary changes in cerebral blood flow**, leading to these symptoms.

B. Sleep Disturbances and Fatigue

- EM signals, particularly **blue light and RF radiation**, may disrupt **melatonin production**, leading to **poor sleep quality, insomnia, and daytime fatigue**.

- Poor sleep can result in **impaired cognitive function, slower reflexes, and difficulty concentrating**.

C. Electromagnetic Hypersensitivity (EHS)

- Some individuals claim to experience **hypersensitivity to EM exposure**, reporting symptoms such as **nausea, tingling, brain fog, and chronic fatigue**.

- While EHS is not formally recognized as a medical condition, some studies suggest that **psychological stress responses** to EM exposure may contribute to these symptoms.

3. Long-Term Effects on the Nervous System

A. Increased Risk of Neurodegenerative Diseases

- Prolonged exposure to **high-intensity EM fields** has been linked to **increased risks of neurodegenerative diseases** like **Alzheimer's, Parkinson's, and ALS (Amyotrophic Lateral Sclerosis)**.

- The mechanism is thought to involve **chronic oxidative stress**, leading to **progressive nerve damage**.

B. Cognitive Decline and Memory Impairment

- Some research suggests that **long-term exposure to EM radiation** may lead to **subtle changes in memory, attention span, and reaction time**.

- Studies on animals exposed to chronic RF radiation have shown **alterations in hippocampal function**, an area of the brain responsible for memory formation.

C. Peripheral Nerve Damage

- The **peripheral nervous system (PNS)**, which controls motor and sensory functions, may also be affected by EM exposure.

- Some studies report **nerve demyelination**, where the protective covering (myelin sheath) around nerves deteriorates, leading to symptoms like **numbness, tingling, or muscle weakness.**

4. Mechanisms of EM Impact on the Nervous System

A. Blood-Brain Barrier (BBB) Disruption

- The **blood-brain barrier (BBB)** is a protective filter that prevents toxins from entering the brain.
- Research suggests that prolonged exposure to **EMFs**, especially from **mobile phones and wireless devices**, might **weaken the BBB**, allowing harmful substances to enter the brain.
- This could contribute to **inflammation, neurotoxicity, and an increased risk of neurodegenerative diseases.**

B. Calcium Ion Channel Disruption

- EM radiation may **interfere with calcium ion channels** in nerve cells, leading to excessive **calcium influx.**
- This can trigger **neurotoxic effects**, such as increased free radical production and nerve cell damage.

C. Altered Brainwave Activity

- Some studies suggest that **RF radiation exposure** can **alter brainwave patterns**, including **alpha, beta, and delta waves**, which are associated with cognitive functions, relaxation, and sleep.
- Disruptions in brainwave activity could explain symptoms like **brain fog, difficulty concentrating, and sleep disturbances.**

5. Protective Measures for the Nervous System

A. Reducing EM Exposure

- **Limit screen time**, especially before bed, to prevent

brain overstimulation and sleep disruption.

- **Use wired connections** instead of wireless when possible (e.g., Ethernet instead of Wi-Fi).

- **Keep mobile phones away from the head** while sleeping or using them for long calls (use speakerphone or wired earphones).

B. Enhancing Antioxidant Defense

- A diet rich in **antioxidants (Vitamin C, Vitamin E, flavonoids, and Omega-3 fatty acids)** can help counteract **oxidative stress** caused by EM exposure.

- **Regular physical exercise** improves blood circulation and helps flush out free radicals that may accumulate due to **EM-induced oxidative stress**.

C. EM Shielding Techniques

- Use **EMF shielding** materials like **special fabrics, paints, and grounding mats** to reduce EM exposure in homes and workplaces.

- **Maintain a safe distance** from high-intensity EM sources such as Wi-Fi routers, power lines, and microwave ovens.

Conclusion

While more research is needed, **growing evidence suggests that long-term exposure to EM radiation may impact the nervous system**, potentially leading to **cognitive impairments, sleep disturbances, neurodegenerative diseases, and nerve damage**. Implementing **protective strategies** can help minimize risks and support **neurological health**.

ELECTROMAGNETIC HYPERSENSITIVITY (EHS): UNDERSTANDING EM SENSITIVITY

What is Electromagnetic Hypersensitivity (EHS)?

Electromagnetic Hypersensitivity (EHS), also known as **Idiopathic Environmental Intolerance attributed to Electromagnetic Fields (IEI-EMF)**, is a condition where individuals report **adverse health effects** due to exposure to electromagnetic (EM) fields. While EHS is not officially recognized as a medical disorder by organizations such as the **World Health Organization (WHO)**, many individuals claim to experience **physical and psychological symptoms** when exposed to EM radiation from devices like mobile phones, Wi-Fi routers, power lines, and even LED lights.

Symptoms of Electromagnetic Hypersensitivity

Symptoms of EHS vary widely among individuals and can be classified into **neurological, dermatological, cardiovascular, and systemic symptoms**.

1. Neurological Symptoms

- Headaches and migraines

- Dizziness and vertigo
- Brain fog and cognitive difficulties
- Memory loss
- Anxiety and depression
- Sleep disturbances (insomnia, poor sleep quality)

2. Dermatological Symptoms

- Tingling or burning sensations on the skin
- Redness, rashes, or inflammation
- Itching or a feeling of heat in specific areas

3. Cardiovascular Symptoms

- Heart palpitations or irregular heartbeat
- Increased or decreased blood pressure
- Chest pain

4. Systemic Symptoms

- Chronic fatigue
- Muscle and joint pain
- Nausea and digestive issues
- Increased sensitivity to light and sound

Possible Causes of EHS

Although no direct **biological mechanism** has been confirmed, several theories attempt to explain why some people report **EHS symptoms**:

1. Increased Sensitivity of the Nervous System

- Some studies suggest that **prolonged exposure to EM fields** may **sensitize the nervous system**, making certain individuals more reactive.
- The **autonomic nervous system (ANS)**, which regulates involuntary functions like heart rate and

stress response, may become overactive in EHS sufferers.

2. Oxidative Stress and Cellular Damage

- EM exposure has been linked to **increased oxidative stress**, which may lead to cellular damage.
- High levels of **reactive oxygen species (ROS)** can cause **inflammation and neurological symptoms**.

3. Blood-Brain Barrier (BBB) Disruption

- Some studies suggest that EM radiation may **weaken the blood-brain barrier**, allowing toxins to enter the brain and cause **neurological disturbances**.

4. Placebo Effect or Nocebo Effect

- Some experts argue that **EHS symptoms may be psychosomatic**, meaning they arise due to **stress, anxiety, or belief that EM radiation is harmful** (Nocebo effect).
- Controlled studies have found that individuals claiming EHS often do not react when they are **unaware** they are being exposed to EM fields.

Scientific Evidence on EHS

- **World Health Organization (WHO)**: Acknowledges that EHS symptoms are real but states that no clear scientific link between EM radiation and symptoms has been established.
- **European Commission's SCENIHR Report (2015)**: Found **no conclusive evidence** that EM fields cause EHS, though some individuals are highly sensitive.
- **Swedish Research**: Sweden recognizes EHS as a functional impairment rather than a disease, offering support to affected individuals.

While mainstream science remains skeptical, some studies

suggest that **low-frequency electromagnetic fields (ELF-EMF)** may have **biological effects**, particularly on the **nervous system and oxidative stress levels**.

How to Manage Electromagnetic Hypersensitivity?

1. Reducing EM Exposure

- **Use wired internet connections** instead of Wi-Fi.
- **Limit mobile phone use** and use speakerphone or wired headsets.
- **Turn off wireless devices** (Wi-Fi routers, Bluetooth) at night.
- **Use EM shielding materials**, such as **radiation-blocking fabrics, paints, and grounding mats**.

2. Improving Sleep Environment

- Keep electronic devices **out of the bedroom**.
- Use an **EMF-free sleeping zone** by turning off power sources near the bed.
- Try **blue-light-blocking glasses** to reduce exposure before sleep.

3. Enhancing Biological Resilience

- **Increase antioxidant intake** (Vitamin C, Vitamin E, Omega-3s) to combat oxidative stress.
- **Regular exercise** to support circulation and detoxification.
- **Meditation and stress reduction techniques** to calm the nervous system.

4. Seeking Medical & Psychological Support

- Some individuals benefit from **functional medicine approaches** focusing on detoxification.
- **Cognitive Behavioral Therapy (CBT)** has been used to manage symptoms in some cases.

Conclusion

While **Electromagnetic Hypersensitivity (EHS)** is not yet scientifically proven as a direct effect of EM radiation, the **reported symptoms are real** and can severely impact quality of life. More research is needed to understand the connection between **EM exposure, neurological function, and chronic health conditions**. Until then, **reducing exposure, enhancing biological resilience, and managing stress** can help those who believe they are affected.

EFFECT OF EM SIGNALS ON ANIMALS: IMPACT ON WILDLIFE (BIRDS, BEES, AND OTHER INSECTS)

Electromagnetic (EM) signals, primarily from human-made sources like cell towers, Wi-Fi, and electrical grids, can have **significant effects on wildlife**, particularly on **birds, bees, and other insects**. While scientific studies are ongoing, emerging research suggests that EM radiation may **disrupt navigation, communication, reproduction, and immune functions** in these species.

---

1. Effect of EM Radiation on Birds

Birds rely heavily on **Earth's natural electromagnetic fields** for navigation, migration, and foraging. Human-made EM signals can **interfere with their internal compass**, leading to:

A. Disrupted Migration Patterns

- Many bird species, such as **pigeons, sparrows, and migratory songbirds**, use the **Earth's geomagnetic field** to navigate.

- Studies have shown that exposure to **radiofrequency (RF) radiation** from cell towers and high-voltage power lines **disorients birds**, leading to **migration delays, route deviations, and population declines**.
- A 2014 study in Germany found that birds exposed to weak **AM radio signals (1-5 MHz)** lost their ability to orient properly.

B. Reduced Reproductive Success

- EM radiation has been linked to **lower hatching rates** and **weakened eggshells** in some bird species.
- Chronic exposure to EM fields may **reduce sperm quality** and increase **genetic mutations** in bird embryos.

C. Increased Stress and Behavioral Changes

- Birds exposed to high levels of EM radiation exhibit **higher stress hormone (cortisol) levels**, leading to:
  - **Aggressive behavior**
  - **Decreased feeding efficiency**
  - **Weakened immune systems**

D. Physical Effects on Feathers and DNA Damage

- Some studies suggest that EM radiation **heats up bird feathers**, leading to **stress and changes in body temperature regulation**.
- Long-term exposure has been linked to **DNA damage and oxidative stress**, which can accelerate aging and disease susceptibility.

2. Effect of EM Radiation on Bees and Pollinators

Bees and other pollinators play a **crucial role in food production** and biodiversity. Recent studies indicate that **radiofrequency (RF) and microwave (MW) radiation** from cell towers and 5G networks may harm **bee behavior, colony health, and survival** rates.

A. Disruption of Navigation and Colony Collapse Disorder (CCD)

- Bees use the **Earth's natural electromagnetic field** for orientation and hive navigation.
- EM radiation **alters their ability to navigate**, leading to **foraging failures and colony collapse disorder (CCD)**.
- A 2017 study found that honeybees exposed to RF fields **lost their ability to return to their hive**, reducing colony survival rates.

B. Reduced Foraging and Pollination Efficiency

- EM signals affect bees' **antennae and sensory systems**, making it harder for them to find flowers and pollinate effectively.
- Studies show that bees exposed to mobile phone signals exhibit **reduced waggle dance activity**, a key communication method for foraging.

C. Genetic and Reproductive Effects

- Exposure to EM radiation increases **oxidative stress**, leading to **DNA damage and reduced sperm viability** in male bees.
- Reduced reproductive success can lead to **population declines and weaker colonies**.

D. Immune System Weakening

- Bees exposed to EM radiation show **higher levels of stress proteins**, making them more susceptible to **pesticides, pathogens, and environmental toxins**.

3. Effect of EM Radiation on Other Insects

A. Disorientation and Reduced Survival Rates

- Many insects, such as **butterflies, ants, and beetles**, use electromagnetic cues for **movement and survival**.
- Studies suggest that EM exposure affects their **ability to detect natural electric fields**, leading to **disorientation and habitat loss**.

B. Cellular and DNA Damage

- High-frequency EM radiation, particularly **from 5G networks**, has been linked to **increased oxidative stress and DNA mutations** in insects.
- This can lead to **deformities, shortened lifespans, and population declines**.

C. Impact on Communication and Reproduction

- Insects like ants use **pheromones and electrical signals** to communicate. EM radiation **interferes with these signals**, leading to **disrupted social behavior and colony breakdown**.
- Some species experience **reduced egg production and lower hatching rates** under constant EM exposure.

4. Broader Ecological Consequences

The decline of birds, bees, and insects due to EM exposure can have **cascading effects on ecosystems**:

- **Loss of pollinators** can lead to **reduced crop yields and food shortages**.
- **Bird population declines** can disrupt the balance of **predator-prey relationships**.
- **Disruption of insect populations** can affect **soil health, plant growth, and biodiversity**.

5. Potential Solutions and Mitigation Strategies

A. Reducing EM Pollution in Sensitive Areas

- Establishing **EM-free zones** in wildlife-rich habitats.

- Restricting **cell tower installations** near bird migration routes and pollinator habitats.

- Implementing **low-radiation technology** in environmentally sensitive areas.

B. Shielding and Protective Measures

- Using **EM shielding materials** on **power lines and communication towers** to reduce radiation spread.

- Developing **bio-compatible wireless technologies** with minimal impact on wildlife.

C. Promoting Research and Awareness

- Encouraging **scientific studies** to understand EM impact on biodiversity.

- Raising public awareness about the **effects of EM radiation on wildlife** and promoting responsible technology use.

Conclusion

Electromagnetic signals have a **significant impact on birds, bees, and insects**, affecting **navigation, reproduction, immune function, and survival rates**. The decline of these species poses **serious ecological risks**, including food shortages and biodiversity loss. While more research is needed, adopting **protective measures and sustainable technology practices** can help mitigate these effects and preserve wildlife.

EFFECT OF EM SIGNALS ON ANIMALS: IMPACT ON DOMESTICATED ANIMALS

Electromagnetic (EM) signals, emitted by various human-made sources such as **Wi-Fi, mobile networks, power lines, and household electronic devices**, have been increasingly scrutinized for their potential effects on domesticated animals. While scientific studies on this topic are still evolving, anecdotal evidence and emerging research suggest that prolonged exposure to EM radiation may cause **behavioral changes, stress, reproductive issues, and potential health concerns** in pets and livestock.

1. Effect of EM Radiation on Household Pets (Dogs, Cats, and Small Mammals)

A. Behavioral Changes and Anxiety

- Domesticated animals, particularly **dogs and cats**, are highly sensitive to changes in their environment, including **subtle electromagnetic fields (EMFs)**.

- Some studies suggest that exposure to **high-frequency EM radiation** can lead to:

- ○ **Increased anxiety and restlessness**
- ○ **Unexplained aggression or behavioral changes**
- ○ **Altered sleep patterns**
- Pets may **avoid certain areas** of the house where Wi-Fi routers or electronic devices are active, indicating possible discomfort from EM exposure.

B. Sleep Disturbances

- Just like humans, **melatonin production** in pets can be disrupted by prolonged EM exposure, leading to **insomnia or irregular sleep cycles**.
- Melatonin is crucial for **immune function and overall well-being**, and disturbances can lead to long-term health effects.

C. Potential Neurological Effects

- Some anecdotal reports suggest that EM exposure could **trigger seizures** in epileptic pets, though more research is needed to confirm a direct link.
- Cats, in particular, may show **twitching, excessive grooming, or unusual vocalizations** when exposed to high EM fields.

D. Immune System and Cellular Stress

- EM radiation has been associated with **oxidative stress**, which can weaken the immune system and increase susceptibility to diseases in pets.
- Prolonged exposure may lead to **chronic inflammation, fatigue, and metabolic changes**.

2. Effect of EM Radiation on Livestock (Cattle, Sheep, Poultry, and Horses)

A. Reduced Milk Production in Dairy Cattle

- Studies have suggested that cows exposed to high

levels of EM radiation, particularly from nearby power lines or cellular towers, experience:

- ○ **Reduced milk yield**
- ○ **Changes in milk composition** (lower fat and protein content)
- ○ **Increased stress and restlessness**

- This may be linked to **hormonal imbalances** caused by EM-induced physiological stress.

B. Reproductive Health Issues

- EM fields can affect **sperm quality and fertility** in livestock, leading to:
  - ○ **Lower conception rates in cows and sheep**
  - ○ **Reduced hatchability in poultry eggs**
  - ○ **Increased incidence of birth defects** in newborn animals

- This effect is thought to be due to **disruptions in hormonal cycles and genetic damage** from prolonged EM exposure.

C. Behavioral Changes and Stress Response

- Horses and cattle may exhibit **increased nervousness and erratic behavior** when near **power lines or radio towers**.

- Animals sensitive to EM fields may show **reluctance to enter certain barns, pastures, or stables** with high EM exposure.

D. Immune Suppression and Increased Disease Susceptibility

- Just like in humans, chronic exposure to EM radiation can lead to **weakened immunity** in livestock, making them more vulnerable to:
  - ○ **Infections**
  - ○ **Metabolic disorders**
  - ○ **Slow wound healing**

3. Impact on Poultry (Chickens, Ducks, and Other Birds)

A. Reduced Egg Production and Hatchability

- Studies indicate that prolonged exposure to EM radiation from power lines and mobile towers **reduces egg-laying capacity** in chickens.

- Hatchability rates may decline due to **genetic damage in embryos** caused by continuous exposure to non-ionizing radiation.

B. Growth and Developmental Issues

- Some research suggests that chicks hatched in high-EM environments may have:
  - **Lower body weights**
  - **Weaker bone structures**
  - **Higher mortality rates**

C. Behavioral and Neurological Effects

- Chickens exposed to high EM fields have shown **increased aggression, restlessness, and abnormal pecking behavior**.

- Possible **disruption of circadian rhythms** due to **altered melatonin levels**, similar to mammals.

4. Broader Ecological and Economic Implications

A. Economic Losses for Farmers

- Lower milk yields, reduced fertility, and weakened livestock health could lead to **significant financial losses** in the dairy, poultry, and meat industries.

- The decline in reproductive efficiency may **increase breeding costs** and reduce overall productivity.

B. Ethical Concerns in Animal Welfare

- If EM exposure is found to have severe long-term effects, there may be increased **pressure on industries** to develop **low-EM farming solutions**.

- Protecting livestock from EM pollution may become a key part of **future sustainable farming practices**.

5. Potential Solutions and Mitigation Strategies

A. Reducing EM Exposure in Animal Housing

- **Keeping Wi-Fi routers and mobile towers away from barns and stables**
- Using **wired internet connections** instead of wireless where possible
- **Reducing the use of high-frequency electric fences and tracking devices**

B. Providing EM Shielding and Safe Zones

- **Grounding barns and stables** to minimize EM radiation exposure
- Installing **EM shielding materials** in walls or enclosures
- Keeping animals **away from high-voltage power lines** and **cellular transmission sites**

C. Monitoring and Regulation

- Encouraging **research on safe EM exposure limits for domesticated animals**
- Implementing **guidelines for farm and pet owners** on minimizing EM exposure
- Advocating for **EM-free zones** in agricultural and rural areas

Conclusion

The increasing presence of electromagnetic radiation in modern environments may **affect domesticated animals**, leading to **behavioral changes, sleep disturbances, immune suppression,**

and reproductive issues. While more research is needed, **implementing protective measures** in both household and agricultural settings can help minimize potential risks.

EFFECT OF EM SIGNALS ON ANIMALS: DISRUPTION OF NAVIGATION & MIGRATION IN BIRDS AND MARINE LIFE

Electromagnetic (EM) signals interfere with the natural navigation abilities of birds, marine animals, and other migratory species. Many animals rely on the Earth's **natural geomagnetic field** for orientation, migration, and foraging. The growing presence of **man-made EM fields**—from power lines, mobile networks, radar systems, and communication satellites —has raised concerns about its **disruptive effects on wildlife migration and survival.**

1. Impact on Birds and Their Navigation Systems

A. Role of Earth's Magnetic Field in Bird Migration

- Birds use a **biological compass**—a magnetoreception system that helps them detect the Earth's magnetic field for navigation.

- This system allows them to maintain precise routes over long distances, even in low visibility conditions.

B. Disruption by Man-Made EM Radiation

- Research suggests that EM fields from urban infrastructure can **interfere with magnetoreception**, leading to:
  - **Disorientation in migratory birds**
  - **Increased risk of getting lost or deviating from migration routes**
  - **Delayed or failed migrations**
- Birds exposed to high EM pollution (e.g., from power lines or radio towers) show **erratic flight patterns and confusion**.

C. Collisions with Man-Made Structures

- Disoriented birds are more likely to **collide with buildings, communication towers, and wind turbines**, leading to increased mortality.
- **Artificial lighting combined with EM pollution** worsens the issue, as birds are attracted to urban lights and lose their natural course.

D. Reduced Survival Rates

- Failure to reach breeding or feeding grounds due to EM-related disorientation can result in:
  - **Population declines**
  - **Weakened genetic diversity**
  - **Decreased reproductive success**

2. Impact on Marine Life (Whales, Dolphins, Sea Turtles, and Fish)

A. Magnetoreception in Marine Species

- Many marine animals, including **whales, dolphins, sharks, and sea turtles**, rely on **geomagnetic cues** for long-distance migration.

- They use **Earth's magnetic field for navigation** in deep waters where visual cues are limited.

B. Disruption by Underwater EM Pollution

- **Submarine cables, sonar systems, offshore wind farms, and military radars** emit EM fields that can distort natural geomagnetic signals.
- Disrupted marine navigation can cause:
  - **Mass strandings of whales and dolphins**
  - **Erratic swimming behavior**
  - **Inability to locate breeding or feeding grounds**

C. Mass Strandings of Whales and Dolphins

- Some studies suggest that **military sonar and underwater communication signals** interfere with marine mammals' **echolocation and magnetoreception**.
- Large-scale strandings have been reported near areas with high naval activity, indicating a strong correlation with EM pollution.

D. Effects on Fish Migration and Breeding

- Fish species such as **salmon and eels** use magnetic fields to return to spawning grounds.
- Man-made EM fields from **hydroelectric dams and power transmission lines** can **alter their migration paths**, leading to:
  - **Declining fish populations**
  - **Disrupted aquatic ecosystems**

3. Effects on Sea Turtles

A. Disrupted Hatchling Orientation

- Sea turtles hatch on beaches and use **natural**

geomagnetic imprints to navigate back to the ocean.

- Coastal EM pollution, including **cell towers, power grids, and artificial lights**, can:
  - Confuse hatchlings, causing them to move **in the wrong direction**.
  - Increase predation risks as disoriented hatchlings become more vulnerable.

B. Challenges in Returning to Nesting Sites

- Female turtles rely on **geomagnetic cues** to return to their birthplace for nesting.
- EM interference may disrupt this natural cycle, reducing **successful reproduction rates**.

4. Broader Ecological Consequences

- **Disrupted migration patterns can lead to ecological imbalances**, affecting predator-prey relationships and food chains.
- Birds and marine species play crucial roles in **pollination, seed dispersal, and maintaining healthy ecosystems**.
- A decline in migratory species can cause **ripple effects throughout entire ecosystems**.

5. Possible Solutions & Conservation Efforts

A. Reducing EM Pollution in Wildlife Habitats

- **Limiting the expansion of high-frequency communication networks in sensitive ecosystems.**
- **Designing low-EM transmission lines** in migratory corridors.

B. Wildlife-Friendly Infrastructure

- **Modifying power lines and wind farms** to minimize EM interference.

- **Using shielding technology** to reduce underwater EM emissions.

C. Monitoring & Research

- Investing in studies on the long-term **effects of EM pollution on migratory species**.
- Implementing **global regulations** to reduce EM interference in critical wildlife habitats.

Conclusion

Electromagnetic signals are emerging as an invisible but significant **threat to migratory birds and marine life**. Disrupting magnetoreception can lead to **navigation failures, population declines, and ecological imbalances**. To protect wildlife, there is an urgent need for **responsible technology development and conservation efforts**.

EFFECT OF EM SIGNALS ON ANIMALS: LABORATORY STUDIES ON EM EXPOSURE IN ANIMALS

Scientific studies have examined the biological effects of electromagnetic (EM) exposure on animals under controlled laboratory conditions. These studies provide valuable insights into how EM radiation, especially from modern communication technologies, affects different biological systems in animals.

---

1. Purpose of Laboratory Studies on EM Exposure

- To understand **short-term and long-term effects** of EM signals on animal physiology and behavior.

- To investigate potential **health risks, including DNA damage, oxidative stress, and reproductive issues**.

- To explore the mechanisms of **EM-induced biological effects**, such as thermal and non-thermal impacts.

- To evaluate the relevance of animal findings to **human health and environmental policies**.

2. Common Animal Models Used in EM Studies

Laboratory studies primarily use the following animals due to their **biological similarity to humans** and controlled breeding conditions:

- **Rodents (rats and mice):** Frequently used to study EM effects on the brain, nervous system, and reproduction.
- **Birds (pigeons, chickens):** Studied for EM impact on navigation and embryonic development.
- **Insects (bees, ants):** Examined for behavioral changes due to EM field exposure.
- **Fish and amphibians:** Used to assess aquatic EM field effects.

3. Major Findings from Laboratory EM Exposure Studies

A. EM Effects on the Nervous System and Brain Function

- Studies on **rats and mice** exposed to mobile phone radiation (900 MHz – 2.4 GHz) show:
  - **Altered neurotransmitter levels**, leading to increased stress and anxiety-like behavior.
  - **Changes in sleep patterns** and cognitive function impairment.
  - Possible **neuronal damage due to oxidative stress** in the brain.
- In birds, prolonged exposure to **radiofrequency (RF) signals** has been linked to **disoriented behavior** and changes in brain wave activity.

B. Impact on DNA and Cellular Health

- Several studies report **DNA damage in rodent cells**

after prolonged exposure to EM fields:
- **Increased levels of DNA strand breaks** in brain and blood cells.
- **Higher oxidative stress markers**, which may lead to premature aging and cancer risks.
- **Disruptions in cellular repair mechanisms**, raising concerns about long-term exposure risks.

- Chick embryo studies indicate that exposure to high-frequency EM fields may cause **abnormal cell division and developmental defects**.

C. Effects on Reproductive Health and Fertility

- Male rats exposed to **mobile phone radiation for 4-6 hours daily** showed:
  - **Reduced sperm count and motility**.
  - **Changes in testosterone levels**, affecting reproductive functions.
  - **Increased testicular oxidative stress**, potentially leading to infertility.
- Female rats exposed during pregnancy exhibited:
  - **Delayed fetal development** and reduced birth weight.
  - **Higher rates of miscarriages** and developmental abnormalities in offspring.

D. EM Radiation and Cardiovascular Effects

- Some rodent studies suggest **heart rate variability** and mild blood pressure changes after prolonged exposure to EM fields.

- EM radiation may cause **slight thickening of blood vessel walls**, increasing the risk of cardiovascular diseases.

E. Behavioral and Cognitive Changes

- Rats and mice exposed to Wi-Fi frequencies (2.4 GHz) showed:
  - **Reduced memory retention and learning ability**.
  - **Increased anxiety and hyperactivity**.
  - Changes in the **expression of brain proteins linked to neurodegenerative diseases**.
- Bees exposed to EM fields (50 Hz–2.4 GHz) displayed:
  - **Reduced foraging ability** and difficulty returning to their hive.
  - **Altered communication patterns**, affecting colony survival.

F. Immune System Alterations

- Some studies suggest **weakened immune responses** in animals after prolonged EM exposure:
  - **Decreased white blood cell count**, making animals more susceptible to infections.
  - **Inflammatory markers increase**, leading to chronic immune system activation.

4. Key Challenges and Controversies in EM Research

- **Variability in study results:** Not all studies confirm harmful effects, leading to ongoing scientific debates.
- **Differences in exposure duration and intensity:** Some studies use high EM doses that may not reflect real-world exposure.
- **Lack of large-scale, long-term studies:** The long-term effects of low-dose EM exposure remain unclear.
- **Species differences:** Effects observed in rodents may not always apply to humans or other animals.

5. Future Research Directions and Safety Recommendations

- More **long-term studies** with standardized exposure

conditions.

- Investigating the effects of **5G and higher-frequency EM fields**.

- Evaluating **potential protective measures**, such as antioxidants and EM shielding materials.

- Establishing global safety guidelines based on **comprehensive animal and human data**.

Conclusion

Laboratory studies provide crucial insights into the biological effects of EM exposure, highlighting potential risks such as **neurological disorders, reproductive issues, and immune system alterations**. However, further research is needed to confirm these findings and **establish safe EM exposure limits for both animals and humans**.

EFFECT OF EM SIGNALS ON PLANTS & MICROORGANISMS: EM EXPOSURE AND PLANT GROWTH

Electromagnetic (EM) radiation can influence plant growth, development, and metabolism. While plants do not have nervous systems like animals, they still respond to external environmental stimuli, including electromagnetic fields (EMFs). Research on the effects of EM signals on plants has yielded mixed results, with both **positive and negative effects** depending on factors like **frequency, intensity, and duration of exposure**.

1. Mechanisms of EM Interaction with Plants

Plants interact with EM radiation primarily through:

- **Absorption of EM waves** by water, pigments (like chlorophyll), and cellular structures.
- **Induction of reactive oxygen species (ROS)**, which can cause oxidative stress.
- **Changes in ion transport and cellular signaling**, affecting metabolism and growth.

2. Impact of EM Radiation on Plant Growth and Development

A. Positive Effects of EM Radiation on Plants

Some studies indicate that low-intensity EM exposure can **stimulate plant growth**:

1. **Increased Germination Rates**
   - Weak EM fields (low-frequency waves) have been shown to **speed up seed germination** in some plant species.
   - Example: Exposure to **50 Hz electromagnetic fields** improved the germination of wheat and soybean seeds.

2. **Enhanced Photosynthesis**
   - Certain EM frequencies can **increase chlorophyll production**, leading to better photosynthesis and faster growth.
   - Example: **Radio frequency waves (RF: 900 MHz)** were observed to increase the biomass of some crops.

3. **Improved Water Uptake and Root Growth**
   - Low-level EM fields may **stimulate root elongation** and **enhance water absorption**, leading to improved drought resistance.

B. Negative Effects of EM Radiation on Plants

On the other hand, excessive or high-frequency EM radiation has been found to **inhibit plant growth**:

1. **Reduced Germination and Growth Delays**
   - Prolonged exposure to high-intensity EM radiation (such as mobile tower radiation) can **slow down seed germination and plant growth**.
   - Example: Studies on **tomato and maize seeds**

showed delayed germination when exposed to high-frequency EM fields.

2. **Oxidative Stress and Cellular Damage**
   - High-frequency EM radiation can cause **oxidative stress**, leading to **cellular damage and reduced growth**.
   - Example: **Wi-Fi radiation (2.4 GHz)** increased oxidative stress markers in plant cells, leading to stunted growth.

3. **Changes in Nutrient Uptake**
   - EM fields can interfere with **ion transport**, leading to **altered nutrient absorption** in plants.
   - Example: Studies on wheat and barley indicate **reduced nitrogen and potassium uptake** after prolonged exposure to EM fields.

4. **Altered Flowering and Reproductive Cycles**
   - Some plants exposed to prolonged EM radiation exhibit **delayed flowering or reduced seed production**.
   - Example: **Sunflower plants exposed to EM fields showed lower seed viability** and reduced pollen production.

3. Real-World Observations of EM Impact on Plants

A. Effects of Mobile Tower Radiation on Urban Vegetation

- **Trees near mobile towers** often show **asymmetrical leaf damage**, slower growth, and premature leaf fall.
- Some reports suggest that trees exposed to **continuous high-frequency radiation** suffer from **dehydration and reduced chlorophyll levels**.

B. Effects of High-Voltage Power Lines on Agricultural Crops

- Farmers near **high-voltage transmission lines** have reported **lower crop yields and weaker plant structures**.
- Some experiments indicate that **high electromagnetic fields near power lines alter plant hormone levels**, affecting growth.

4. Future Research and Mitigation Strategies

A. Need for Further Research

- More long-term studies are required to understand the exact **mechanisms of EM impact on plant biology**.
- Research on **genetically modifying plants to resist EM radiation effects** is an emerging field.

B. Mitigation Techniques

- **Using shielding materials (like mesh or conductive barriers)** around sensitive crops.
- **Adjusting planting distances from EM sources** (e.g., mobile towers and power lines).
- **Exploring electromagnetic therapy for plants**, where controlled EM exposure is used to **boost plant immunity**.

Conclusion

The effects of EM exposure on plant growth vary based on frequency, intensity, and duration. While **low-intensity EM radiation may enhance growth**, high-frequency and prolonged exposure **can cause oxidative stress, reduced germination, and nutrient imbalances**. As technology advances, further research is needed to determine safe EM exposure levels for plant ecosystems and agricultural productivity.

EFFECT OF EM SIGNALS ON PLANTS & MICROORGANISMS: IMPACT ON SEED GERMINATION AND CROP YIELD

Electromagnetic (EM) signals have been found to influence **seed germination and crop yield**, either positively or negatively, depending on factors such as **frequency, intensity, duration of exposure, and plant species**. While some studies suggest that certain EM fields can **stimulate seed germination and enhance crop yield**, prolonged exposure to high-frequency radiation may lead to **growth inhibition, cellular damage, and reduced agricultural productivity**.

1. Effect of EM Signals on Seed Germination

Seed germination is a critical phase in a plant's life cycle, influenced by environmental factors such as moisture, temperature, and radiation. EM radiation can impact germination in multiple ways:

A. Positive Effects on Seed Germination

Certain frequencies of EM radiation have been observed to

enhance seed germination rates and improve early-stage growth in some plant species:

1. **Accelerated Germination Process**
   - Low-frequency EM fields (50 Hz–100 Hz) have been reported to **stimulate enzyme activity** in seeds, promoting **faster water absorption and metabolic activation**.
   - Example: Studies on **wheat, barley, and maize seeds** have shown that controlled exposure to weak EM fields increases germination rates.

2. **Increased Root and Shoot Length**
   - Exposure to **low-intensity radiofrequency waves** has been linked to **improved root elongation and shoot development**, leading to healthier seedlings.
   - Example: **Sunflower and tomato seeds** exhibited **stronger root growth** when exposed to specific EM frequencies.

3. **Enhanced Seed Viability**
   - Weak EM exposure can **reduce seed dormancy** and improve **germination uniformity**, especially in aged or stressed seeds.
   - Example: **Soybean seeds exposed to low-intensity EM fields** showed better germination even under drought conditions.

B. Negative Effects on Seed Germination

High-frequency or prolonged EM exposure may **inhibit seed germination** and **disrupt early plant development**:

1. **Delayed Germination or Reduced Germination Rates**
   - High-intensity EM fields (e.g., from **mobile phone towers and high-voltage power**

lines) can **damage seed DNA and cellular structures**, leading to **slower germination or reduced viability**.

- Example: **Lettuce and mustard seeds exposed to mobile tower radiation** had lower germination rates compared to unexposed seeds.

2. **Altered Water Uptake and Enzyme Activity**
   - Strong EM fields can **interfere with the water absorption process**, making it difficult for seeds to break dormancy.
   - Example: **Corn and rice seeds exposed to high-frequency EM radiation** exhibited **reduced amylase enzyme activity**, slowing starch breakdown needed for germination.

3. **Structural and Genetic Damage**
   - High-frequency radiation can induce **mutations and chromosomal aberrations**, potentially leading to **weak seedlings or malformed plants**.
   - Example: Some **experimental studies on barley and soybean seeds** showed DNA fragmentation after prolonged EM exposure.

2. Effect of EM Signals on Crop Yield

Crop yield is directly linked to seed germination, plant health, and reproductive success. EM radiation can influence **growth rate, flowering, fruiting, and nutrient uptake**, leading to variations in yield.

A. Positive Effects on Crop Yield

Certain controlled EM exposure has been reported to **boost agricultural productivity** under the right conditions:

1. **Improved Growth Rate and Biomass Production**

- Weak EM fields can enhance **photosynthesis efficiency**, leading to **larger biomass and higher crop productivity**.

- Example: **Experiments with rice and wheat crops** showed an increase in grain yield under controlled EM exposure.

2. **Resistance to Stress Factors**

   - Some studies suggest that pre-treating seeds with EM radiation can **increase resistance to drought, salinity, and extreme temperatures**.

   - Example: **Tomato and soybean plants exposed to weak EM waves** showed improved resistance to **water stress conditions**.

B. Negative Effects on Crop Yield

Prolonged or high-intensity EM radiation may result in **yield reduction** due to various physiological and biochemical disruptions:

1. **Reduced Flowering and Fruit Production**

   - Continuous exposure to **high-frequency EM radiation (e.g., Wi-Fi, mobile networks)** has been linked to **hormonal imbalances**, affecting the flowering and fruiting stages of crops.

   - Example: **Strawberry and bell pepper plants** showed reduced flower production when exposed to strong EM fields.

2. **Altered Nutrient Uptake and Metabolism**

   - EM fields can **disrupt ion transport channels**, affecting **nutrient absorption and photosynthesis efficiency**.

   - Example: **Corn and sunflower plants**

exhibited reduced **nitrogen and phosphorus uptake**, leading to poor growth and lower yields.

3. **Weaker Plant Structure and Susceptibility to Disease**
   - Prolonged exposure can weaken plant cell walls, making crops more **vulnerable to pests, fungal infections, and bacterial diseases**.
   - Example: **Cucumber and lettuce plants** exposed to strong EM fields showed increased susceptibility to fungal infections.

3. Real-World Observations of EM Impact on Agriculture

A. Effects of Mobile Tower Radiation on Crop Fields

- Farmers near **cell phone towers** have reported **stunted crop growth and lower fruit yields**, particularly in orchards and vegetable farms.
- Some studies indicate that EM exposure from **4G and 5G towers** affects **pollination rates**, reducing crop yield.

B. Impact of Power Lines on Large-Scale Farming

- **High-voltage transmission lines** running across agricultural lands have been linked to **lower wheat and maize yields** due to prolonged exposure to **electric and magnetic fields**.

4. Mitigation Strategies for Sustainable Agriculture

A. Protective Measures

1. **Using Shielding Materials**
   - Planting crops behind **natural barriers (trees, hills) or using metallic mesh** can reduce EM exposure.

2. **Increasing Distance from EM Sources**
   - Farmers should **avoid planting highly sensitive crops** near **mobile towers or power lines.**

3. **Seed Pre-Treatment with EM Fields**
   - Controlled exposure to **low-frequency EM waves** before planting may improve germination and resilience.

4. **Bioengineering and Genetic Modification**
   - Research is being conducted to develop **EM-resistant crop varieties** for better agricultural sustainability.

Conclusion

Electromagnetic radiation plays a complex role in **seed germination and crop yield**, with both **potential benefits and risks.** While **low-intensity EM exposure** may improve germination, stimulate growth, and enhance yield, **high-frequency and prolonged exposure** can lead to **delayed germination, poor crop health, and lower agricultural productivity.** Further research is required to **develop agricultural practices that mitigate harmful EM exposure while leveraging its benefits** for sustainable farming.

EFFECT OF EM SIGNALS ON PLANTS & MICROORGANISMS: EM EFFECTS ON BACTERIA AND OTHER MICROORGANISMS

Electromagnetic (EM) signals influence **bacteria, fungi, and other microorganisms**, affecting their **growth, reproduction, metabolism, and resistance**. The impact depends on the **frequency, intensity, and duration of exposure**. Some studies suggest **EM radiation can alter bacterial behavior, disrupt microbial ecosystems, and even induce antibiotic resistance**, while others indicate **controlled exposure can be used for sterilization and microbial growth enhancement**.

1. Effects of EM Radiation on Bacteria

Bacteria, being **unicellular organisms**, are highly sensitive to environmental changes, including **electromagnetic fields (EMFs) and radiation**. The effects of EM exposure on bacteria can be classified into **growth stimulation, inhibition, genetic changes, and antibiotic resistance**.

A. Growth Stimulation and Metabolic Changes

Certain **low-intensity EM fields** can **stimulate bacterial growth and metabolism** by affecting cellular respiration and enzymatic activity.

1. **Increased Growth Rates**
   - Studies show that **radiofrequency (RF) and extremely low-frequency (ELF) EM fields** can enhance bacterial reproduction.
   - Example: **E. coli and Lactobacillus** exhibited **faster growth** under weak EM exposure.

2. **Enhanced Biofilm Formation**
   - EM radiation may enhance **biofilm production**, increasing bacterial resistance to antibiotics.
   - Example: **Pseudomonas aeruginosa** exposed to EM waves developed stronger biofilms, making it harder to eliminate.

3. **Metabolic Activity Alterations**
   - Some bacteria exhibit **higher ATP production** when exposed to **weak EM fields**, leading to increased energy metabolism.

B. Growth Inhibition and Cellular Damage

While weak EM exposure can promote bacterial growth, **high-intensity radiation (such as UV, X-rays, and microwaves)** can **damage bacterial DNA, disrupt protein synthesis, and kill bacteria**.

1. **DNA Damage and Mutation Induction**
   - High-frequency EM radiation (e.g., X-rays, gamma rays) can **cause mutations in bacterial DNA,** leading to lethal damage or adaptation.
   - Example: Some studies indicate **gamma radiation exposure can cause mutations in**

Salmonella that make them more resilient.

2. **Membrane Disruption and Structural Damage**
   - **Microwave and ultraviolet (UV) radiation** can **break down bacterial cell membranes**, leading to cell death.
   - Example: **Sterilization techniques using UV light** effectively eliminate **E. coli, Staphylococcus, and Salmonella** on medical surfaces.

3. **Reduced Colony Formation**
   - Certain EM frequencies suppress **bacterial colony formation**, affecting microbial ecosystems.
   - Example: **Exposure to strong Wi-Fi signals (2.4 GHz, 5 GHz) led to reduced bacterial colony formation in lab studies.**

C. Induction of Antibiotic Resistance

One of the most concerning effects of EM exposure is its potential to **trigger antibiotic resistance in bacteria**, which can lead to **treatment failures in infections**.

1. **Increased Resistance Genes Expression**
   - EM exposure may enhance the **expression of antibiotic resistance genes (ARGs)** in bacteria.
   - Example: **E. coli and Staphylococcus aureus** exposed to EM fields showed increased resistance to antibiotics like **penicillin and ampicillin.**

2. **Horizontal Gene Transfer (HGT) Enhancement**
   - Studies suggest that **EM fields can facilitate gene transfer between bacterial populations**, spreading antibiotic resistance.

- Example: **Bacteria exposed to EM radiation in hospital settings** showed increased rates of horizontal gene transfer.

2. Effects of EM Radiation on Other Microorganisms

Besides bacteria, EM radiation also impacts **fungi, viruses, and protozoa**, influencing their growth, reproduction, and pathogenicity.

A. Effects on Fungi and Mold

Fungi, such as **yeast and mold**, exhibit varying responses to EM radiation.

1. **Enhanced Fungal Growth**
   - Certain low-frequency EM fields **increase fungal spore germination and colony expansion**.
   - Example: **Aspergillus and Penicillium molds** grew faster under weak EM exposure.

2. **UV and Microwave-Induced Fungal Inhibition**
   - High-intensity UV and microwave radiation can **destroy fungal spores**, preventing mold contamination.
   - Example: **UV-C light is used in air purification systems to kill airborne fungal spores**.

B. Effects on Viruses

Viruses are **smaller than bacteria and fungi**, and their interaction with EM radiation is less understood.

1. **Potential for Genetic Mutations**
   - High-energy radiation (UV, X-rays) can **cause mutations in viral RNA/DNA**, possibly weakening or enhancing virulence.

- Example: **UV light is used for viral disinfection** in medical settings.

2. **Altered Infection Potential**
    - Some studies suggest EM fields **may influence viral replication rates**, though findings remain inconclusive.

C. Effects on Protozoa and Algae

Protozoa and algae, important for ecological balance, can be affected by EM fields.

1. **Increased Growth in Some Algae**
    - Weak EM exposure can enhance **chlorophyll production**, leading to **higher algal growth rates**.
    - Example: **Microalgae used for biofuel production respond positively to controlled EM exposure.**

2. **Suppressed Protozoa Growth**
    - Some protozoa, like **Paramecium and Giardia**, exhibit **slower reproduction rates** under strong EM fields.

3. Real-World Implications of EM Effects on Microorganisms

A. Public Health Concerns

- **Rise in antibiotic-resistant bacteria** due to EM exposure poses serious health risks.
- **Hospitals and laboratories** need to assess EM field exposure to prevent microbial adaptation.

B. Agricultural and Environmental Implications

- EM radiation may alter **soil microbial communities**, affecting **nutrient cycling and plant health**.
- Overexposure may lead to **imbalanced ecosystems**,

disrupting natural microbial interactions.

C. Industrial Applications

- **Controlled EM radiation is used in sterilization**, food preservation, and wastewater treatment.
- **UV sterilization in hospitals and food processing plants** ensures microbial safety.

4. Mitigation Strategies and Future Research

A. Controlling EM Exposure in Sensitive Areas

- Limiting unnecessary **Wi-Fi and cell tower radiation** near hospitals, farms, and research labs.
- Using **shielding materials** in critical environments.

B. Enhancing Research on Microbial Responses

- More studies needed on **long-term EM effects on bacterial resistance and microbial ecology**.
- Investigating the use of **low-intensity EM fields for microbial growth control** in agriculture.

C. Utilizing EM for Beneficial Applications

- Using controlled **radiofrequency waves to stimulate beneficial microbes** in biofertilizers.
- Developing **UV-based sterilization** methods for safer food processing.

Conclusion

EM signals have **a significant impact on bacteria, fungi, viruses, and other microorganisms,** influencing **growth, resistance, and genetic stability.** While **controlled EM exposure** can be **beneficial for sterilization and microbial applications,** uncontrolled exposure may **increase antibiotic resistance and disrupt ecosystems.** More research is required to **balance technological advancements with microbial health**

and safety.

EFFECT OF EM SIGNALS ON PLANTS & MICROORGANISMS: CHANGES IN SOIL MICROBIOTA AND ECOSYSTEM BALANCE

Electromagnetic (EM) signals influence **soil microbiota**, impacting the **composition, diversity, and function of microorganisms** that are essential for soil health and ecosystem balance. Soil microorganisms, including **bacteria, fungi, archaea, and protozoa**, play a crucial role in **nutrient cycling, organic matter decomposition, and plant health**. Changes induced by EM exposure can lead to **imbalances in microbial populations**, potentially affecting **soil fertility, crop productivity, and overall ecosystem stability**.

1. Role of Soil Microbiota in Ecosystem Balance

Soil microbiota contribute to **multiple ecological functions** that sustain plant life and environmental stability:

- **Nutrient Cycling:** Decomposition of organic matter and conversion of **nitrogen, phosphorus, and carbon** into forms accessible to plants.

- **Symbiotic Relationships: Rhizobacteria and mycorrhizal fungi** aid in plant growth and disease resistance.

- **Decomposition & Carbon Sequestration:** Breakdown of plant and animal residues into **humus**, regulating soil structure.

- **Disease Suppression:** Beneficial microbes help **control plant pathogens** and maintain a balanced microbial community.

EM exposure can disrupt these functions, altering the **microbial ecosystem balance** and potentially leading to negative consequences.

2. Impact of EM Radiation on Soil Microbial Communities

The effects of EM signals on soil microbes depend on factors such as **frequency, intensity, duration of exposure, and soil composition**.

A. Changes in Microbial Diversity and Abundance

- Some studies show **declining bacterial and fungal populations** in soil exposed to strong EM fields.

- Beneficial microbes like **Nitrobacter and Mycorrhizal fungi** may decrease, affecting soil fertility.

- Certain microbes, like **pathogenic bacteria and antibiotic-resistant strains**, may thrive under EM exposure.

B. Disruption of Nitrogen-Fixing Bacteria

- **Rhizobia bacteria**, responsible for nitrogen fixation in legumes, show **reduced activity** under EM exposure.

- Lower nitrogen availability can **weaken plant growth and reduce crop yields.**

C. Altered Microbial Metabolism and Enzymatic Activity

- EM fields can affect **soil enzymes** involved in organic matter breakdown.

- Enzymes like **urease and phosphatase**, essential for nutrient cycling, show **reduced activity** in EM-exposed soils.

D. Soil Fungi and Mycorrhizae Disruption

- **Mycorrhizal fungi**, which form symbiotic relationships with plant roots, may be **negatively affected**, reducing their ability to help plants absorb nutrients.

- Fungal species that support **soil structure and decomposition** could decline, leading to **poorer soil quality**.

3. Effects of EM Fields on Soil Health and Plant Growth

A. Reduced Soil Fertility

- Disruption of microbial functions **lowers nutrient availability**, impacting plant health.

- Loss of **decomposers and nitrogen-fixing bacteria** leads to **lower organic matter content**.

B. Increased Soil Pathogen Activity

- Some studies suggest that **EM fields may favor harmful pathogens**, increasing plant disease risks.

- Example: **Fusarium and Pythium**, which cause root rot, have shown increased growth under EM exposure.

C. Water Retention and Soil Structure Changes

- Soil microbial activity helps maintain **moisture levels** by improving soil aggregation.

- EM-induced microbial disruptions may lead to **poor soil structure and water retention**, making soil prone to **erosion and drought stress**.

4. Long-Term Ecological Implications

A. Effects on Soil-Plant Interactions

- Reduced microbial support **weakens plant resistance** to environmental stress.
- Lower **nutrient uptake efficiency** could lead to **lower crop yields** in agricultural lands.

B. Disruption of Carbon and Nitrogen Cycles

- Imbalanced microbial activity could slow **carbon sequestration**, contributing to **climate change**.
- Nitrogen cycle disruption can cause **soil acidification**, affecting long-term land fertility.

C. Biodiversity Loss in Ecosystems

- A decline in soil microbial diversity may **affect higher trophic levels**, such as **earthworms, insects, and larger animals** that rely on soil health.

5. Mitigation Strategies and Sustainable Solutions

A. Reducing EM Exposure in Agricultural and Natural Areas

- **Strategic placement of cell towers and power lines** to minimize exposure in sensitive soil environments.
- Using **EM shielding materials** around agricultural zones.

B. Restoring Microbial Communities

- Introducing **biofertilizers and compost** to replenish beneficial soil microbes.
- Using **probiotic bacteria** to counteract EM-induced microbial imbalances.

C. Enhancing Soil Protection Measures

- Encouraging **no-till farming, crop rotation, and cover crops** to maintain microbial balance.

- Reducing **chemical fertilizers and pesticides**, which may compound EM effects.

D. Further Research and Monitoring

- Conducting **long-term field studies** to understand how different **EM frequencies** impact soil health.
- Developing **EM-resistant microbial strains** to maintain soil balance.

6. Conclusion

Electromagnetic signals can **alter soil microbial communities**, affecting **nutrient cycles, plant growth, and ecosystem balance**. While some microbes may **adapt or thrive**, many beneficial species decline, leading to **reduced soil fertility and increased plant disease susceptibility**. By implementing **sustainable agricultural practices and minimizing unnecessary EM exposure**, we can **mitigate negative effects and protect soil health** for future generations.

ELECTROMAGNETIC RADIATION AND PUBLIC HEALTH CONCERNS: REGULATORY GUIDELINES AND SAFETY LIMITS

Electromagnetic (EM) radiation is an integral part of modern life, emitted by various sources such as **cell towers, mobile phones, Wi-Fi routers, power lines, and medical imaging devices**. While EM radiation is essential for communication and technology, its potential health risks have led to the development of **regulatory guidelines and safety limits** to **protect public health**.

1. Need for Regulatory Guidelines

As scientific research explores the effects of **long-term EM exposure**, health organizations and governments worldwide have implemented **safety limits** to:

Minimize potential health risks such as **thermal effects, non-thermal effects, and electromagnetic hypersensitivity (EHS)**.

Ensure that EM emissions from electronic devices **do not exceed harmful levels**.

Guide industries in designing **safe and compliant** technology.

2. Key Organizations Setting EM Radiation Standards

Several national and international organizations regulate **EM radiation exposure limits** to ensure **public and occupational safety**:

A. International Organizations

1. **International Commission on Non-Ionizing Radiation Protection (ICNIRP)**
   - Develops exposure guidelines for **radiofrequency (RF), microwave, and low-frequency EM fields**.
   - Provides **recommended limits** based on scientific studies.

2. **World Health Organization (WHO)**
   - Conducts research on **health effects of EM radiation**.
   - Works with ICNIRP to **evaluate risks and update safety limits**.

3. **Institute of Electrical and Electronics Engineers (IEEE)**
   - Sets standards for **wireless communication and power transmission safety**.
   - Works with the **Federal Communications Commission (FCC)** on exposure guidelines.

4. **International Agency for Research on Cancer (IARC)**
   - A part of WHO that classified **radiofrequency (RF) radiation as "possibly carcinogenic" (Group 2B)** in 2011.

B. National Regulatory Agencies

1. **Federal Communications Commission (FCC) – USA**
   - Sets **RF exposure limits** for mobile phones, cell towers, and Wi-Fi.
   - Uses **Specific Absorption Rate (SAR) limits** to regulate devices.

2. **European Union (EU) – Council Recommendation 1999/519/EC**
   - Adopts **ICNIRP guidelines** for public EM exposure limits.
   - Enforces regulations for **telecommunications, power grids, and consumer electronics**.

3. **Indian Council of Medical Research (ICMR) & Department of Telecommunications (DoT) – India**
   - Adopted **ICNIRP standards** and imposed **stringent EMF limits** for mobile towers.

4. **China, Russia, and Eastern Europe**
   - Have **stricter RF limits** than ICNIRP, imposing **lower exposure levels**.

3. Safety Limits for Electromagnetic Exposure

A. Specific Absorption Rate (SAR) Limits

SAR measures **how much EM energy is absorbed by the body** when exposed to a radiofrequency device.

Region	SAR Limit (W/kg) for Mobile Devices
USA (FCC)	1.6 W/kg (averaged over 1g of tissue)
EU (ICNIRP)	2.0 W/kg (averaged over 10g of tissue)
India (DoT)	1.6 W/kg (same as FCC)

Devices exceeding SAR limits are restricted from sale.

B. Exposure Limits for Radiofrequency (RF) Radiation

Frequency Range	ICNIRP Public Exposure Limit	Occupational Limit
50 Hz (Power Lines)	100 μT (microtesla)	500 μT
3 kHz – 10 MHz	2 V/m – 87 V/m	6 V/m – 614 V/m
30 MHz – 300 GHz (Mobile Networks, Wi-Fi, Radar)	0.08 W/m² – 10 W/m²	0.4 W/m² – 50 W/m²

Occupational exposure limits are higher because workers in certain industries use **protective measures**.

4. Regulatory Measures and EMF Safety Guidelines

A. Mobile Towers and Wi-Fi Regulation

- Governments impose **maximum transmission power** for mobile towers.
- Some countries enforce **minimum distance requirements** between **residential areas and cell towers**.
- **Wi-Fi routers** have power limits to **reduce excessive EM exposure** in homes and offices.

B. Consumer Electronics & Wireless Devices

- **SAR testing** is required before selling mobile phones, tablets, and Bluetooth devices.
- Regulations **restrict high-power RF transmitters** in residential areas.

C. EMF Shielding and Safe Design

- Use of **shielded cables, grounding, and radiation-reducing materials** in power lines and electronic devices.
- Smart city planning includes **low-EMF zones** in schools and hospitals.

D. Public Awareness and Safety Campaigns

- Governments and health agencies promote **safe mobile phone usage**:
  Use **wired headphones or speaker mode** to reduce head exposure.
  Keep **mobile phones away from the body** when not in use.
  Limit **long conversations** or use **text messaging** instead.

5. Controversies and Ongoing Debates

Despite safety guidelines, some experts argue that:
Current exposure limits may not be strict enough to protect against **long-term non-thermal effects**.
Some studies link EM radiation to **sleep disorders, cognitive issues, and neurological effects**, requiring **more research**.
The **5G rollout** has raised concerns about **higher-frequency millimeter waves**, though ICNIRP states it is safe within limits.

6. Future Research & Evolving Regulations

Advancements in EM research will shape **future safety standards**.
Some countries may **tighten EMF regulations** based on **new health findings**.
New shielding technologies may improve **EM safety in consumer electronics**.

7. Conclusion

Regulatory guidelines and safety limits are **critical** in **protecting public health** from excessive EM radiation. While **current limits** set by ICNIRP, FCC, and national agencies provide **general safety**, ongoing research will help refine standards to **address long-term exposure risks**.

ELECTROMAGNETIC RADIATION AND PUBLIC HEALTH CONCERNS: WHO AND INTERNATIONAL STANDARDS ON EM EXPOSURE

Electromagnetic radiation (EMR) has become an integral part of modern society, but its potential health effects have sparked ongoing discussions. The **World Health Organization (WHO)** and international standards set by organizations like **ICNIRP (International Commission on Non-Ionizing Radiation Protection)** play crucial roles in regulating EM exposure to protect public health. Here's a detailed look into the WHO's involvement and the global standards on EM exposure.

1. WHO's Role in EMR Research and Public Health

The **World Health Organization (WHO)** is the primary global body responsible for public health and safety, including the assessment and regulation of environmental factors like electromagnetic radiation. WHO's involvement in EM radiation is based on:

A. Research and Health Risk Assessment

- **WHO's International Agency for Research on Cancer (IARC)** has **classified radiofrequency electromagnetic fields** (RF-EMF) as **possibly carcinogenic to humans (Group 2B)** in 2011, based on evidence linking prolonged mobile phone usage to **brain tumors**.

- WHO works closely with researchers worldwide to **monitor, assess, and analyze the scientific evidence** on potential health effects from EMR, including **thermal and non-thermal impacts**.

B. Formulating Guidelines and Recommendations

- WHO **provides public health guidelines** on EM exposure, based on the recommendations from **ICNIRP** and other international scientific bodies.

- WHO regularly updates its **health advisories** regarding **safe exposure limits** to EM fields, reflecting the latest scientific evidence.

C. EMF Project

- The **WHO EMF Project** is an initiative aimed at reducing the health risks associated with exposure to **non-ionizing radiation** (like EM waves).

- This project focuses on:
  - **Reviewing research** and conducting **risk assessments**.
  - Providing **evidence-based recommendations** for **safe exposure**.
  - Developing **public health communication strategies** to inform people about EM safety.

D. EMF and Public Awareness Campaigns

- WHO supports national and international campaigns to **raise awareness** about **safe use of mobile phones** and other wireless technologies to reduce potential risks from excessive EM exposure.

- It also works with governments to implement **protective measures** and **regulations** related to EM radiation.

2. International Standards for EM Exposure

Several global organizations have developed **standards and guidelines** to regulate EM exposure in different environments. The aim is to prevent health risks and ensure safety, especially for vulnerable populations such as children and pregnant women.

A. International Commission on Non-Ionizing Radiation Protection (ICNIRP)

- **ICNIRP**, an independent organization, provides **scientific advice and guidance** on the health effects of non-ionizing radiation, including **radiofrequency (RF)** and **extremely low-frequency (ELF)** electromagnetic fields.

ICNIRP Guidelines:

- **General public exposure limits** are designed to avoid **thermal effects** (such as tissue heating) from exposure to EM fields.

- **Occupational limits** are higher because workers often use safety protocols.

Exposure Limits by ICNIRP:

Frequency Range	Public Exposure Limit	Occupational Exposure Limit
50/60 Hz (Power Lines)	100 μT (microtesla)	500 μT
300 Hz – 3 GHz (Mobile, Wi-Fi,	0.08 W/m^2 – 10 W/m^2	0.4 W/m^2 – 50 W/m^2

Broadcasting)

3 GHz – 300 GHz (5G, Radar)	0.08 W/m² – 10 W/m²	0.4 W/m² – 50 W/m²

These limits are set **to prevent thermal effects**, but **non-thermal effects** are still being researched.

B. Federal Communications Commission (FCC) – USA

The **FCC** in the United States sets **specific absorption rate (SAR)** limits for mobile devices to ensure **safe use**. For mobile phones, the **SAR limit** is **1.6 W/kg**, averaged over 1 gram of tissue.

- The FCC also enforces guidelines to prevent **electromagnetic interference** in communications and broadcasts.

C. European Union (EU)

The **European Union** follows **ICNIRP** guidelines and has regulations in place to **protect public health** from **electromagnetic radiation**.

- The **EU Directive 2013/35/EU** sets out limits for **workplace exposure** to **EM fields** for workers, providing guidelines for safe EM exposure in **occupational environments**.
- The **European Commission** reviews new scientific data and recommends **policy adjustments** to ensure that **EM exposure levels** in public areas are kept within safe limits.

D. Other National Regulations

Different countries have set their **national standards** based on **international guidelines** and the **specific health concerns** of their population.

- **India:** The **Department of Telecommunications (DoT)** has set **SAR limits** and has introduced **guidelines to** control EM exposure from mobile towers.

- **Australia and New Zealand:** These countries adopt ICNIRP's standards for **RF exposure limits** and have national bodies like **ARPANSA** (Australian Radiation Protection and Nuclear Safety Agency) that oversee **EM radiation** exposure in workplaces and public spaces.

3. Ongoing Challenges and Considerations

A. Mobile Phones and Long-Term Exposure

- Despite **existing standards**, concerns continue about the long-term effects of **mobile phone radiation**, especially given the rise of **smartphones** and **5G technologies**.

- Some studies suggest links between **EM radiation** and conditions such as **brain tumors, sleep disturbances**, and **cognitive issues**.

- The **non-thermal effects** of EM radiation are **still under investigation**, and the **WHO** continues to update its recommendations as more data becomes available.

B. Public Perception and Electromagnetic Hypersensitivity (EHS)

- The rise in **EHS** (a condition where individuals report sensitivity to EM fields) raises questions about whether more stringent exposure limits are necessary.

- WHO supports **research into EHS** but stresses that no **clear biological mechanisms** have been identified to explain the symptoms.

C. Emerging Technologies and Their Impact

- **5G and the Internet of Things (IoT)** are expected to bring about **higher frequencies** and **denser networks** of EM exposure.

- These technologies raise concerns about whether current guidelines adequately protect against **new forms of radiation**.

4. Conclusion

The **WHO** and **international regulatory bodies** such as **ICNIRP** play an essential role in maintaining **public health** by setting **safe EM radiation exposure limits**. While **current guidelines** are based on existing research, the **rapid advancement in EM technology**, particularly with the advent of **5G networks** and the **increased use of wireless devices**, calls for continued **monitoring, research**, and **updated standards**. Ensuring **long-term safety** will require constant **collaboration** between **scientists, health organizations, governments**, and **industry stakeholders** to protect human health while fostering technological innovation.

ELECTROMAGNETIC RADIATION AND PUBLIC HEALTH CONCERNS: CONTROVERSIES AND ONGOING RESEARCH

The topic of **electromagnetic radiation (EMR)** and its potential effects on human health has been the subject of considerable debate and controversy for many years. While the majority of research has focused on **ionizing radiation** (such as X-rays and gamma rays) due to their well-documented health risks, **non-ionizing radiation** (such as radiofrequency radiation from mobile phones, Wi-Fi, and power lines) is often less clearly understood, leading to divided opinions within the scientific community, regulators, and the public.

In this chapter, we will explore the **controversies** surrounding the health effects of EM radiation, ongoing research, and the **challenges** faced in forming conclusive public health guidelines.

1. The Controversy: Health Effects of EM Radiation

A. Unclear Evidence on Health Risks

- **Cancer Risk**: One of the central points of contention

is whether **non-ionizing EM radiation** (e.g., from mobile phones and wireless networks) can increase the risk of **cancer**, particularly **brain tumors**. The **International Agency for Research on Cancer (IARC)** classified **radiofrequency electromagnetic fields (RF-EMF)** as **possibly carcinogenic (Group 2B)** in 2011, based on limited evidence of a potential association with **glioma** (a type of brain tumor). This classification has sparked debate between **scientific communities**, with some advocating for further studies and others questioning the significance of the findings.

- **Non-Thermal Effects**: While thermal effects (tissue heating) from high levels of EM radiation are well understood, there is ongoing controversy surrounding **non-thermal effects**, which are subtler and less well-defined. Some studies have suggested that **low-level EM exposure** might influence cellular processes, immune function, or DNA, but **no clear biological mechanism** has been identified to explain such effects. The difficulty in establishing a clear cause-and-effect relationship leads to differing opinions on the potential risks.

B. Public Anxiety vs. Scientific Consensus

- Despite **scientific guidelines** that indicate EM exposure within certain limits is **safe**, there has been growing **public anxiety** and concerns over the **long-term effects** of technologies like **mobile phones, wireless networks**, and **smart meters**. This public perception often clashes with the **scientific consensus**, leading to debates about whether EM exposure is **underestimated** or **overstated**.

- **Electromagnetic Hypersensitivity (EHS)** is another area of controversy. EHS is characterized by self-reported symptoms such as headaches, fatigue, and dizziness, which individuals attribute to EM exposure. Although scientific studies have found **no measurable physical basis** for these symptoms, the condition remains real for many people, adding to the debate over the **biological plausibility** of non-thermal EM effects.

2. Ongoing Research on EM Radiation and Health

Given the **lack of consensus** and **public health concerns**, extensive research is ongoing to better understand the effects of EM radiation on human health. Some of the key areas of ongoing research include:

A. Long-Term Exposure Studies

- **Cohort Studies**: Researchers are conducting long-term **cohort studies** that track large groups of people over decades to observe any potential links between **EM exposure** (such as mobile phone use, proximity to power lines, or living near cell towers) and health outcomes like **cancer, neurological disorders, and cardiovascular disease**. However, the **difficulty** in isolating EM radiation as a singular factor amidst other environmental risks has made these studies challenging.

- **Epidemiological Studies**: Large epidemiological studies such as the **INTERPHONE study**, funded by the **World Health Organization (WHO)**, aim to examine the link between mobile phone use and **brain tumors**. However, results from such studies have been **mixed**, with some showing **slightly elevated risks** and others showing **no correlation**. Researchers are particularly focused on the potential effects of long-term, high-intensity use, particularly among **heavy users** or **younger populations** who are more vulnerable.

B. Non-Thermal Mechanisms of Action

- **Cellular and Molecular Effects**: Ongoing research is focused on understanding whether **low-level EM exposure** can trigger **biological effects** in cells and tissues, even if no thermal heating occurs. Some studies suggest that EM radiation could potentially influence **ion channels**, **gene expression**, **DNA damage**, or **cellular stress responses**, leading to concerns about long-term health effects, such as cancer or neurological disorders.

- **Oxidative Stress**: A significant area of focus is the potential role of EM radiation in inducing **oxidative stress**, which could damage **cells** and **tissues**. Some studies suggest that **RF radiation** could increase the production of **reactive oxygen species (ROS)**, leading to DNA damage and altering cellular functions.

C. Impact on the Nervous System

- **Brain Function and Cognitive Impact**: The effects of EM radiation on the **brain** and **nervous system** remain a highly debated topic. Some studies suggest that chronic exposure to **RF fields** might affect **cognitive function**, **memory**, and **sleep patterns**, particularly in children and adolescents whose brains are still developing. There is concern that **long-term mobile phone use** could affect brain activity and cognition, but studies have not consistently demonstrated these effects.

- **Electromagnetic Hypersensitivity (EHS)**: Research on **EHS** continues as scientists investigate the possible biological mechanisms that could explain the reported symptoms. Some researchers hypothesize that psychological factors, such as **stress** or **anxiety**, may play a significant role in **EHS**, while others are exploring **possible physiological mechanisms** that could explain why certain individuals feel

hypersensitive to EM fields.

D. Animal and Environmental Studies

- Research on the **impact of EM radiation on animals**, especially **wildlife**, is also ongoing. Studies have raised concerns about how **EM exposure** might affect the **navigation**, **behavior**, and **health** of animals like **birds, bees**, and **marine life**. Some animal studies have reported potential changes in **reproductive health**, **growth rates**, or **migration patterns** of certain species, though more research is needed to determine whether these findings are applicable to humans.

E. 5G and the Future of EM Research

- The roll-out of **5G technology** has added a new dimension to EM research, with concerns about higher **frequencies** (from **3 GHz to 300 GHz**) and **denser networks** of **small cells**. While current research on **5G health effects** is still in its early stages, studies are already being conducted to understand how the **higher frequencies** used by **5G** may affect **human health**, **DNA**, and **cellular systems**.

- Researchers are particularly interested in the impact of **5G exposure** on **skin**, **eyes**, and **immune function**, as these body parts may be more directly exposed to radiation from the **smaller, more frequent transmitters**.

---

3. Challenges in EM Radiation Research

Several challenges hinder the ability to definitively answer whether EM radiation poses a health risk:

A. Complexity of Exposure

- EM radiation is **everywhere** and takes many forms. People are exposed to a **wide range of frequencies**, intensities, and durations from sources like **mobile** phones, power lines, Wi-Fi networks, and microwave ovens. This makes it difficult to isolate and measure the effects of individual exposures.

B. Lack of Standardized Research Protocols

- There is no universal agreement on the optimal research protocols for studying EM radiation effects. Different studies use different exposure levels, timeframes, and methodologies, making it hard to compare results. Researchers are calling for standardized experimental models that can be universally adopted.

C. Long Latency Periods

- The potential effects of long-term EM exposure may not become apparent for decades, making it difficult to establish a clear cause-and-effect relationship in a short period. The long latency periods of certain diseases, such as cancer, further complicate the assessment of potential health risks.

4. Conclusion

The debate over the health effects of electromagnetic radiation remains complex and unresolved, with a clear scientific consensus yet to be reached. While existing evidence suggests that exposure within safe limits does not pose significant risks, long-term studies and research into non-thermal effects are critical to providing a clearer understanding of potential health risks.

As technologies evolve, ongoing research will play a crucial role in ensuring public health safety, especially with the advent of new wireless technologies like 5G. Balancing technological innovation with health precautions will require continued collaboration between scientists, regulators, and the public to ensure that the benefits of EM technologies do not come at the expense of human well-being.

ELECTROMAGNETIC RADIATION AND PUBLIC HEALTH CONCERNS: CONTROVERSIES AND ONGOING RESEARCH

The topic of **electromagnetic radiation (EMR)** and its potential effects on human health has been the subject of considerable debate and controversy for many years. While the majority of research has focused on **ionizing radiation** (such as X-rays and gamma rays) due to their well-documented health risks, **non-ionizing radiation** (such as radiofrequency radiation from mobile phones, Wi-Fi, and power lines) is often less clearly understood, leading to divided opinions within the scientific community, regulators, and the public.

In this chapter, we will explore the **controversies** surrounding the health effects of EM radiation, ongoing research, and the **challenges** faced in forming conclusive public health guidelines.

---

1. The Controversy: Health Effects of EM Radiation

A. Unclear Evidence on Health Risks

- **Cancer Risk**: One of the central points of contention

is whether **non-ionizing EM radiation** (e.g., from mobile phones and wireless networks) can increase the risk of **cancer**, particularly **brain tumors**. The **International Agency for Research on Cancer (IARC)** classified **radiofrequency electromagnetic fields (RF-EMF)** as **possibly carcinogenic (Group 2B)** in 2011, based on limited evidence of a potential association with **glioma** (a type of brain tumor). This classification has sparked debate between **scientific communities**, with some advocating for further studies and others questioning the significance of the findings.

- **Non-Thermal Effects**: While thermal effects (tissue heating) from high levels of EM radiation are well understood, there is ongoing controversy surrounding **non-thermal effects**, which are subtler and less well-defined. Some studies have suggested that **low-level EM exposure** might influence cellular processes, immune function, or DNA, but **no clear biological mechanism** has been identified to explain such effects. The difficulty in establishing a clear cause-and-effect relationship leads to differing opinions on the potential risks.

B. Public Anxiety vs. Scientific Consensus

- Despite **scientific guidelines** that indicate EM exposure within certain limits is **safe**, there has been growing **public anxiety** and concerns over the **long-term effects** of technologies like **mobile phones, wireless networks**, and **smart meters**. This public perception often clashes with the **scientific consensus**, leading to debates about whether EM exposure is **underestimated** or **overstated**.

- **Electromagnetic Hypersensitivity (EHS)** is another area of controversy. EHS is characterized by self-reported symptoms such as headaches, fatigue, and dizziness, which individuals attribute to EM exposure. Although scientific studies have found **no measurable physical basis** for these symptoms, the condition remains real for many people, adding to the debate over the **biological plausibility** of non-thermal EM effects.

2. Ongoing Research on EM Radiation and Health

Given the **lack of consensus** and **public health concerns**, extensive research is ongoing to better understand the effects of EM radiation on human health. Some of the key areas of ongoing research include:

A. Long-Term Exposure Studies

- **Cohort Studies**: Researchers are conducting long-term **cohort studies** that track large groups of people over decades to observe any potential links between **EM exposure** (such as mobile phone use, proximity to power lines, or living near cell towers) and health outcomes like **cancer, neurological disorders, and cardiovascular disease**. However, the **difficulty** in isolating EM radiation as a singular factor amidst other environmental risks has made these studies challenging.

- **Epidemiological Studies**: Large epidemiological studies such as the **INTERPHONE study**, funded by the **World Health Organization (WHO)**, aim to examine the link between mobile phone use and **brain tumors**. However, results from such studies have been **mixed**, with some showing **slightly elevated risks** and others showing **no correlation**. Researchers are particularly focused on the potential effects of long-term, high-intensity use, particularly among **heavy users** or **younger populations** who are more vulnerable.

B. Non-Thermal Mechanisms of Action

- **Cellular and Molecular Effects**: Ongoing research is focused on understanding whether **low-level EM exposure** can trigger **biological effects** in cells and tissues, even if no thermal heating occurs. Some studies suggest that EM radiation could potentially influence **ion channels**, **gene expression**, **DNA damage**, or **cellular stress responses**, leading to concerns about long-term health effects, such as cancer or neurological disorders.

- **Oxidative Stress**: A significant area of focus is the potential role of EM radiation in inducing **oxidative stress**, which could damage **cells** and **tissues**. Some studies suggest that **RF radiation** could increase the production of **reactive oxygen species (ROS)**, leading to DNA damage and altering cellular functions.

C. Impact on the Nervous System

- **Brain Function and Cognitive Impact**: The effects of EM radiation on the **brain** and **nervous system** remain a highly debated topic. Some studies suggest that chronic exposure to **RF fields** might affect **cognitive function**, **memory**, and **sleep patterns**, particularly in children and adolescents whose brains are still developing. There is concern that **long-term mobile phone use** could affect brain activity and cognition, but studies have not consistently demonstrated these effects.

- **Electromagnetic Hypersensitivity (EHS)**: Research on **EHS** continues as scientists investigate the possible biological mechanisms that could explain the reported symptoms. Some researchers hypothesize that psychological factors, such as **stress** or **anxiety**, may play a significant role in **EHS**, while others are exploring **possible physiological mechanisms** that could explain why certain individuals feel

hypersensitive to EM fields.

D. Animal and Environmental Studies

- Research on the **impact of EM radiation on animals**, especially **wildlife**, is also ongoing. Studies have raised concerns about how **EM exposure** might affect the **navigation, behavior**, and **health** of animals like **birds, bees**, and **marine life**. Some animal studies have reported potential changes in **reproductive health, growth rates**, or **migration patterns** of certain species, though more research is needed to determine whether these findings are applicable to humans.

E. 5G and the Future of EM Research

- The roll-out of **5G technology** has added a new dimension to EM research, with concerns about higher **frequencies** (from **3 GHz to 300 GHz**) and **denser networks** of **small cells**. While current research on **5G health effects** is still in its early stages, studies are already being conducted to understand how the **higher frequencies** used by **5G** may affect **human health, DNA**, and **cellular systems**.

- Researchers are particularly interested in the impact of **5G exposure** on **skin, eyes**, and **immune function**, as these body parts may be more directly exposed to radiation from the **smaller, more frequent transmitters**.

3. Challenges in EM Radiation Research

Several challenges hinder the ability to definitively answer whether EM radiation poses a health risk:

A. Complexity of Exposure

- EM radiation is **everywhere** and takes many forms. People are exposed to a **wide range of frequencies**, intensities, and durations from sources like **mobile**

phones, power lines, Wi-Fi networks, and **microwave ovens**. This makes it difficult to isolate and measure the effects of **individual exposures**.

B. Lack of Standardized Research Protocols

- There is no universal agreement on the **optimal research protocols** for studying EM radiation effects. Different studies use different **exposure levels**, **timeframes**, and **methodologies**, making it hard to compare results. Researchers are calling for **standardized experimental models** that can be universally adopted.

C. Long Latency Periods

- The potential effects of long-term EM exposure may not become apparent for **decades**, making it difficult to establish a clear cause-and-effect relationship in a short period. The long latency periods of certain diseases, such as **cancer**, further complicate the assessment of potential health risks.

4. Conclusion

The **debate over the health effects of electromagnetic radiation** remains complex and unresolved, with a clear **scientific consensus** yet to be reached. While **existing evidence** suggests that exposure within safe limits does not pose significant risks, **long-term studies** and research into **non-thermal effects** are critical to providing a clearer understanding of potential health risks.

As **technologies evolve**, ongoing research will play a crucial role in ensuring **public health safety**, especially with the **advent of new wireless technologies** like **5G**. Balancing technological innovation with **health precautions** will require continued collaboration between **scientists, regulators**, and **the public** to ensure that the benefits of EM technologies do not come at the expense of **human well-being**.

ELECTROMAGNETIC POLLUTION AND ENVIRONMENTAL IMPACT: SOURCES OF EM POLLUTION

Electromagnetic pollution, also known as **electrosmog**, is the unintended release of **electromagnetic radiation (EMR)** from various human-made sources. As modern technology advances, the levels of **electromagnetic field (EMF) exposure** in the environment have significantly increased. While EM radiation has numerous applications in communication, healthcare, and industry, its uncontrolled spread has raised concerns about potential environmental and health impacts.

In this section, we will explore the **primary sources of electromagnetic pollution**, including their characteristics and areas of concern.

1. Mobile Towers and Base Stations

A. Characteristics of Mobile Towers

- Mobile towers, also known as **cell towers or base stations**, are essential for providing **wireless communication services** for mobile phones and other wireless devices.

- These towers emit **radiofrequency (RF) radiation** in the **300 MHz to 100 GHz** range, depending on the technology (**2G, 3G, 4G, and 5G**).
- As network demand grows, the number of mobile towers is increasing, leading to concerns about **constant exposure** to RF radiation.

B. Environmental Concerns

- **Wildlife Impact**: Some studies suggest that prolonged RF exposure may interfere with the **navigation abilities of birds** and the **behavior of insects** such as bees.
- **Electromagnetic Interference**: High concentrations of RF fields from cell towers can interfere with **other electronic equipment**, leading to signal disruptions.
- **Public Health**: Concerns exist over prolonged exposure to RF radiation, especially for people living close to mobile towers.

2. Wi-Fi Networks and Wireless Devices

A. Characteristics of Wi-Fi Radiation

- **Wi-Fi routers and hotspots** emit **radiofrequency radiation** in the **2.4 GHz and 5 GHz bands** (with newer standards using higher frequencies like **6 GHz**).
- These signals enable wireless communication between **smartphones, laptops, tablets, and IoT devices**.

B. Environmental and Health Concerns

- **Constant Low-Level Exposure**: Unlike mobile towers, which are positioned at a distance, **Wi-Fi routers** are commonly found in homes, offices, and public places, leading to **constant exposure** at close range.
- **Effect on Plants and Microorganisms**: Some studies indicate that Wi-Fi radiation could influence **plant**

growth, seed germination, and microbial activity in soil.

- **Electromagnetic Hypersensitivity (EHS)**: Some individuals report experiencing **headaches, fatigue, and sleep disturbances** when exposed to Wi-Fi signals, though scientific evidence remains inconclusive.

3. Radar Systems

A. Characteristics of Radar Radiation

- Radar systems use **high-frequency electromagnetic waves** (typically **1 GHz – 100 GHz**) to detect and track objects.
- They are used in **airports, military defense, weather monitoring**, and **maritime navigation**.

B. Environmental Impact

- **Aviation and Wildlife**: Radar signals can potentially **disrupt migratory bird patterns**, as birds rely on Earth's natural **electromagnetic fields** for navigation.
- **Marine Life**: Underwater radar (such as **SONAR**) has been linked to **whale and dolphin strandings**, as these species use natural acoustic signals for communication.

4. Power Lines and Electrical Grids

A. Characteristics of Power Line Radiation

- High-voltage **power transmission lines** generate **extremely low-frequency (ELF) electromagnetic fields (EMF)**, typically in the **50–60 Hz range**.
- These fields are present wherever electricity is generated, transmitted, or distributed.

B. Environmental and Health Concerns

- **Long-Term Exposure Risks**: Some epidemiological

studies suggest a possible link between long-term exposure to ELF fields and **childhood leukemia**, but no conclusive evidence has been established.

- **Interference with Wildlife**: Some research indicates that **power line radiation** could affect **birds, bats, and insects**, potentially leading to changes in **migration behavior and reproductive health**.

5. Satellite Communication and Space-Based EM Sources

A. Characteristics of Satellite EM Radiation

- Communication satellites use **microwaves and radio waves** to transmit signals to Earth.
- The increasing deployment of **satellite constellations (e.g., Starlink, OneWeb, GPS satellites)** is contributing to EM radiation in the **atmosphere and outer space**.

B. Environmental Concerns

- **Astronomical Interference**: Radio waves from satellites can interfere with **radio telescopes**, affecting **astronomical observations**.
- **Increased EM Radiation**: The rise in satellite-based communication is increasing global exposure to **RF radiation**, though the impact on health is still under study.

6. Smart Meters and IoT Devices

A. Characteristics of Smart Meters

- **Smart meters** are used for automated reading of electricity, gas, and water consumption.
- They operate on **RF signals (900 MHz to 2.4 GHz)** and are always transmitting data.

B. Public Health and Environmental Concerns

- **Continuous Exposure**: Since smart meters operate

24/7, some residents express concerns about **chronic RF exposure**, particularly in densely populated areas.

- **Privacy and Security Risks**: The wireless nature of smart meters raises concerns about **data privacy and cybersecurity threats**.

7. Electromagnetic Fields in Industrial and Medical Applications

A. Industrial Equipment

- **Induction furnaces, electric motors,** and **high-voltage machinery** emit **low- and mid-frequency EM radiation**.
- **Industrial EM pollution** is concentrated in **factories and workplaces**, affecting workers who spend extended hours near high-powered machinery.

B. Medical EM Sources

- **MRI (Magnetic Resonance Imaging)** and **X-ray machines** use strong **electromagnetic fields** for **medical imaging**.
- **Electromagnetic Therapy** is used for pain relief and **neurological treatments**, but excessive exposure to medical EM radiation could have unintended side effects.

8. Electromagnetic Pollution from Emerging Technologies (5G and Beyond)

A. Characteristics of 5G Radiation

- **5G networks** use a combination of **low-band (600 MHz – 1 GHz), mid-band (1 GHz – 6 GHz),** and **high-band (millimeter waves, 24 GHz – 100 GHz)** for faster communication.
- Unlike previous networks, **5G relies on smaller,**

densely packed base stations, increasing EM exposure in cities.

B. Public and Environmental Concerns

- **Higher Frequencies, More Exposure**: The use of millimeter waves (**mmWave**) in 5G raises concerns about its effects on **human skin, eyes, and immune systems**.

- **Impact on Birds and Insects**: Some studies suggest that **millimeter waves** could disrupt **honeybee behavior** and other **pollinating insects**.

- **Urban EM Density**: The **deployment of millions of small cell antennas** in urban areas may lead to increased **public exposure** to RF radiation.

Conclusion

The rapid expansion of **wireless technologies, power infrastructure, and industrial applications** has led to an increase in **electromagnetic pollution**. While **scientific research** continues to assess the potential risks, it is crucial to implement **safety measures**, including **regulatory guidelines**, **public awareness**, and **environmentally friendly technological innovations**.

As **EM exposure levels rise**, balancing technological progress with **environmental and public health concerns** will be essential for sustainable development.

ELECTROMAGNETIC POLLUTION AND ENVIRONMENTAL IMPACT: URBAN VS. RURAL EM EXPOSURE DIFFERENCES

Electromagnetic (EM) pollution varies significantly between **urban and rural environments** due to differences in infrastructure, population density, and technological deployment. Urban areas are heavily populated with **wireless networks, mobile towers, and electronic devices**, leading to higher EM exposure. In contrast, rural areas have **fewer sources of EM radiation**, but exposure levels are rising due to expanding connectivity.

This section explores the key **differences in EM exposure** between urban and rural settings, their respective **environmental impacts**, and potential **health concerns**.

---

1. Sources of EM Pollution in Urban vs. Rural Areas

A. Urban Areas (High EM Pollution)

Urban regions have a **dense concentration of EM sources**, including:

- **Cell Towers & 5G Networks**: Numerous base stations and small cells to support high data traffic.
- **Wi-Fi Hotspots**: Offices, homes, shopping malls, and public transport are continuously emitting RF signals.
- **Smart Cities & IoT Devices**: Traffic monitoring systems, smart streetlights, and surveillance cameras contribute to **constant EM radiation**.
- **Industrial & Commercial EM Sources**: High-voltage power lines, factories, and transport systems (e.g., metro, electric vehicles).
- **Medical & Security Equipment**: MRI machines, body scanners, and airport security systems increase **localized exposure**.

Impact: Continuous exposure to high-frequency EM radiation from multiple overlapping sources.

B. Rural Areas (Lower EM Pollution, but Increasing)

Rural regions typically have:

- **Fewer Cell Towers**: Limited network infrastructure results in **lower RF radiation**, but longer exposure to strong signals from distant towers.
- **Limited Wi-Fi Coverage**: Less penetration of wireless internet, reducing cumulative exposure.
- **Agricultural EM Sources**: Use of **satellite communication, irrigation sensors, and automated machinery** contributes to increasing EM presence.
- **Power Lines and Electrical Equipment**: High-voltage transmission lines passing through rural areas emit **low-frequency EM fields (ELF-EMF)**.

Impact: Lower overall exposure but increasing with expanding network infrastructure.

2. Health Effects of Urban vs. Rural EM Exposure

A. Urban Areas: High-Frequency Exposure Risks

- **Chronic EM Exposure**: Prolonged exposure to **high-frequency EM waves (Wi-Fi, 5G, mobile networks)** may contribute to **headaches, sleep disturbances, and cognitive stress**.

- **Electromagnetic Hypersensitivity (EHS)**: Some individuals report symptoms such as **fatigue, dizziness, and skin irritation** due to continuous EM exposure.

- **Impact on Mental Health**: Urban dwellers exposed to multiple EM sources might experience **increased stress and anxiety levels**.

B. Rural Areas: Different EM Risks

- **Long-Distance Mobile Radiation**: In areas with **few cell towers**, mobile phones emit stronger signals to stay connected, leading to **higher localized RF exposure**.

- **Low-Frequency EM Fields (ELF-EMF) from Power Lines**: Some studies suggest a potential link between **chronic ELF-EMF exposure and neurological effects**.

- **Agricultural EM Impact**: Farmers using wireless-controlled machinery are **increasingly exposed** to EM fields, though at a lower intensity than in urban areas.

3. Impact on Wildlife and Ecosystems

A. Urban Areas: Impact on Birds, Insects, and Plants

- **Disruption of Bird Navigation**: High EM radiation from **mobile towers and Wi-Fi networks** may affect birds' ability to **navigate using Earth's magnetic field**.

- **Bee Colony Collapse**: Studies suggest **RF radiation** may interfere with **honeybee communication and**

reproduction, affecting pollination.

- **Altered Plant Growth**: Some research indicates that **Wi-Fi and mobile signals** may slow plant growth and affect **photosynthesis**.

B. Rural Areas: Agricultural and Ecological Impact

- **Crop Yield and Seed Germination**: Some studies show **EM radiation can affect seed germination rates and plant development**.

- **Soil Microbiota Changes**: Continuous exposure to **low-frequency EM fields** may alter **bacterial populations**, affecting soil fertility.

- **Impact on Livestock**: Dairy cows exposed to **high-voltage power lines** show **stress behaviors and reduced milk production** in some studies.

4. Policy and Regulatory Challenges

A. Urban Areas: Managing High-Density EM Pollution

- Governments impose **strict EM radiation limits** for urban regions.

- Adoption of **shielding techniques** (EM filters, smart building designs) to reduce human exposure.

- **Public concern** over 5G deployment due to **higher-frequency exposure**.

B. Rural Areas: Expanding Connectivity with Minimal Impact

- Expansion of **broadband and 5G networks** should consider **environmental impact assessments**.

- Research on **safe EM limits for agricultural and ecological balance**.

- Policies to **reduce unnecessary long-distance RF transmissions** in low-density areas.

Conclusion

Urban areas face **higher EM pollution** due to technological infrastructure, while rural areas have **lower but increasing EM exposure** due to expanding connectivity. Each environment has **unique risks**, and research is ongoing to develop **safer EM management strategies** for **public health and environmental sustainability**.

ELECTROMAGNETIC POLLUTION AND ENVIRONMENTAL IMPACT: ECOLOGICAL BALANCE AND BIODIVERSITY THREATS

Electromagnetic (EM) pollution has **far-reaching effects on ecosystems**, influencing biodiversity, wildlife behavior, and overall ecological balance. With the **increasing presence of mobile towers, satellite networks, Wi-Fi, and power lines**, concerns have risen regarding the impact of electromagnetic radiation (EMR) on plants, animals, and microorganisms.

This section explores how **EM pollution threatens biodiversity**, disrupts **natural ecosystems**, and poses risks to **species survival and ecological stability**.

---

1. Impact on Birds and Their Navigation

Many bird species rely on the **Earth's magnetic field for navigation**, particularly during migration. EM radiation from **cell towers, satellites, and radar stations** can interfere with these natural processes.

- **Disrupted Magnetoreception:** Birds use **magnetoreception** (the ability to detect the Earth's magnetic field) for orientation. Studies suggest that EM signals **interfere with this process**, causing **disorientation and migration errors**.
- **Nest Abandonment:** Areas with high EM exposure (e.g., near mobile towers) have reported **reduced nesting activity** and **decreased bird populations**.
- **Reproductive Decline:** Studies indicate that EM exposure may affect **egg incubation and hatchling survival rates** in some bird species.

Example: Research on **European robins** has shown that weak EM fields from radio towers **disrupt their magnetic compass**, leading to navigation failure.

2. Effects on Insects (Bees, Butterflies, and Pollinators)

Pollinators like **bees and butterflies** play a crucial role in maintaining **biodiversity and food production**. However, EM radiation may negatively impact their behavior and survival.

- **Bee Colony Collapse Disorder (CCD):** EM exposure can interfere with **honeybee communication**, affecting their ability to **find food, return to the hive, and reproduce**.
- **Reduced Pollination Efficiency:** If pollinators struggle to navigate, plants receive fewer visits, leading to **lower crop yields** and disrupted ecosystems.
- **Altered Insect Physiology:** Some studies suggest EM fields can affect **metabolic rates and reproductive cycles** in insects.

Example: A study found that when bees were exposed to **mobile phone radiation**, they **lost their way back to the hive**, increasing colony stress.

3. Impact on Mammals and Larger Wildlife

Large mammals, particularly those sensitive to EM fields, may experience **changes in behavior, reproduction, and stress levels**.

- **Livestock Health Issues**: Dairy cows exposed to **high-voltage power lines** have shown **reduced milk production and altered immune responses**.

- **Wild Mammals Avoiding EM Zones**: Certain species (e.g., deer and wolves) **tend to avoid high-EM areas**, which could disrupt **hunting and migration** patterns.

- **Neurological Stress and Hormonal Changes**: Prolonged EM exposure may trigger **stress responses in mammals**, affecting their **cognitive abilities and overall health**.

Example: Studies on rodents exposed to EM fields show **increased anxiety-like behaviors and changes in brain chemistry**.

4. Effects on Marine Life

Many marine organisms, including **whales, dolphins, and sea turtles**, rely on **natural electromagnetic cues** for migration and hunting. Increased EM pollution from **submarine cables, sonar systems, and undersea communication networks** poses significant threats.

- **Disrupted Navigation in Marine Animals**: Whales and dolphins use **electromagnetic sensitivity** to migrate. EM interference may lead to **strandings and disorientation**.

- **Changes in Fish Behavior**: Some species, like **sharks and rays**, detect weak electric fields to locate prey. Increased EM pollution could **disrupt hunting patterns**.

- **Interference with Coral Reef Growth**: There is ongoing research into whether EM exposure may **affect coral ecosystems and microbe interactions**.

Example: Mass whale strandings have been linked to **sonar and undersea electromagnetic disturbances**.

5. Impact on Plants and Forests

Plants are not immune to EM pollution. EM exposure can influence **growth, photosynthesis, and seed germination**, potentially affecting **entire ecosystems**.

- **Reduced Photosynthetic Activity**: Some studies suggest that EM fields can alter **chlorophyll content**, impacting plant **energy production**.
- **Delayed Seed Germination**: Research indicates that **high-frequency EM radiation** can slow **germination rates** and affect **root development**.
- **Weakened Plant Immunity**: Long-term exposure may make plants **more susceptible to diseases and pests**, affecting overall biodiversity.

Example: Trees near mobile towers have shown **abnormal growth patterns**, such as **bark splitting and premature leaf shedding**.

6. Alteration of Soil Microbiota and Microbial Ecosystems

Soil contains **diverse microbial communities** that are essential for **nutrient cycling, decomposition, and plant health**. EM exposure may disrupt these systems.

- **Reduction in Beneficial Microorganisms**: EM fields could decrease populations of **nitrogen-fixing bacteria**, affecting **soil fertility**.
- **Altered Decomposition Rates**: Changes in microbial communities might **slow or accelerate organic matter breakdown**, impacting **ecosystem balance**.

- **Potential for New Microbial Strains**: Some studies suggest that bacteria exposed to EM radiation may develop **genetic mutations**, influencing their **evolution and resistance patterns**.

Example: Laboratory studies have shown **changes in bacterial growth rates** under prolonged EM exposure.

7. Disruption of Ecological Chains and Biodiversity Loss

The interconnected nature of ecosystems means that **disrupting one species can trigger cascading effects** throughout the environment.

- **Decline in One Species Affects Others**: If pollinators like bees are **negatively impacted**, plants and the animals that rely on them also suffer.
- **Food Chain Imbalance**: If fish and insects behave abnormally due to EM exposure, **predator-prey relationships** may change.
- **Ecosystem Fragmentation**: Avoidance of high-EM areas by animals can lead to **disrupted migration routes and habitat loss**.

Example: A decline in pollinators due to EM exposure could lead to **reduced fruit and vegetable production**, affecting food supply chains.

8. Future Research and Conservation Strategies

Given the rising concern over EM pollution, scientists and environmentalists are working on solutions to **minimize its impact on biodiversity**.

- **Stricter EM Regulations**: Governments and agencies should establish **stricter limits** on EM radiation levels in **protected areas** and near **wildlife habitats**.
- **Eco-Friendly Infrastructure Development**: Using **low-EM communication technologies** and relocating

cell towers away from sensitive areas.

- **Increased Research on EM Ecology**: More studies on **long-term EM exposure effects** on different species are needed to inform policy.

- **Public Awareness & Sustainable Technology Use**: Promoting the **responsible use of wireless technology** to minimize unnecessary EM exposure.

Example: Some countries have proposed **5G-free zones** in **wildlife reserves** to protect **sensitive species**.

Conclusion

Electromagnetic pollution poses **a growing threat to biodiversity**, affecting **birds, insects, marine life, plants, and ecosystems**. While more research is needed, **mitigation strategies**, including **regulations, eco-friendly infrastructure, and conservation policies**, can help **preserve ecological balance** in an increasingly **technologically advanced world**.

STRATEGIES FOR REDUCING ELECTROMAGNETIC POLLUTION

With the increasing prevalence of **mobile networks, Wi-Fi, power lines, satellites, and other electronic devices**, electromagnetic (EM) pollution has become a significant environmental concern. To mitigate its impact on **human health, wildlife, and ecosystems**, several strategies can be implemented at **individual, industry, and policy levels**.

1. Regulatory Measures and Policy Implementation

A. Stricter EM Radiation Limits

- Governments and international agencies (e.g., **WHO, ICNIRP, FCC**) should **enforce stricter exposure limits** for EM emissions from **cell towers, radar, and power lines**.

- Introducing **safe zones** where EM radiation levels remain **below scientifically recommended thresholds**.

- Mandatory **environmental impact assessments (EIA)** before approving large-scale **telecommunication projects**.

B. Creation of Low-EM Zones

- Establishing **low-EM exposure areas** near **schools, hospitals, and wildlife sanctuaries.**

- Restricting **cell towers and Wi-Fi networks** in **ecologically sensitive regions.**

C. Global Standardization of EM Safety Measures

- Different countries have **varying EM exposure limits.** Establishing **universal guidelines** ensures **better safety** across the world.

Example: Some European countries, like **Switzerland and Italy,** have stricter EM exposure limits than global standards.

2. Sustainable Telecommunication Infrastructure

A. Eco-Friendly Network Planning

- Using **low-power transmission antennas** instead of **high-power cell towers** to reduce **EM field intensity.**

- Deploying **fiber-optic networks** as an alternative to **wireless technology,** reducing overall EM radiation.

B. Optimized Placement of Cell Towers

- Avoid placing cell towers **near residential areas, schools, and hospitals.**

- Encouraging **shared network infrastructure** among telecom providers to **reduce the number of towers.**

C. Development of Low-Radiation Devices

- Promoting **energy-efficient mobile devices** that emit **lower radiation.**

- Encouraging manufacturers to design **phones and routers with reduced SAR (Specific Absorption Rate)** values.

Example: Some smartphone brands now feature **low-radiation mode settings** to **reduce user exposure.**

3. Personal and Household Measures

A. Reducing Wireless Device Usage

- Limiting **unnecessary use of Wi-Fi, Bluetooth, and mobile data** when not needed.
- Preferring **wired internet connections (Ethernet)** over **Wi-Fi** for home and office use.
- Using **speaker mode or wired headsets** instead of holding the phone close to the head.

B. Safe Placement of EM-Emitting Devices

- Keeping **Wi-Fi routers away** from bedrooms and living spaces.
- Turning off **wireless devices at night** to reduce exposure.

C. Using EM Shields and Protective Materials

- Installing **low-EM paint, window films, and shielding fabric** to reduce radiation penetration into homes.
- Using **EM-blocking phone cases** to minimize direct exposure to the body.

Example: Some schools in **France and Germany** have **banned Wi-Fi in classrooms** to protect children from prolonged EM exposure.

4. Innovations in EM-Free and EM-Safe Technologies

A. Advanced EM Shielding Techniques

- Developing **shielded cables and enclosures** to prevent EM leaks from power lines and electronics.
- Using **bio-compatible shielding materials** (e.g., graphene-based coatings) to reduce radiation exposure.

B. Alternative Communication Technologies

- Exploring **Li-Fi (Light Fidelity)** as a **safer alternative** to traditional Wi-Fi, as it **relies on light waves** instead of radio waves.

- Using **wired internet and landlines** instead of **wireless networks** in high-EM areas.

Example: Some researchers are exploring **terahertz-based communication** that **reduces harmful EM exposure** while maintaining high data speeds.

5. Protecting Wildlife and Ecosystems

A. EM-Free Zones in Natural Habitats

- Restricting **cell tower construction near forests, national parks, and marine reserves**.
- Banning **high-power radar stations** in wildlife-sensitive areas.

B. Monitoring EM Impact on Biodiversity

- Conducting **long-term studies** on the effect of EM pollution on **birds, bees, marine animals, and plants**.
- Regulating **satellite networks and 5G rollouts** to ensure minimal **environmental impact**.

C. Promoting Sustainable Farming Practices

- Avoiding **EM-intensive agricultural technologies** near sensitive ecosystems.
- Studying the **impact of EM fields on soil microbiota and crop health** before deploying high-tech farming solutions.

Example: Some cities in **India and Spain** have **restricted 5G deployment near beekeeping zones** to protect pollinators.

6. Public Awareness and Education

A. Educating People About EM Pollution

- Spreading awareness about **safe mobile phone use and**

Wi-Fi management.

- Encouraging the use of **EM-safe home designs** with **minimal electronic interference**.

B. Promoting EM-Free Workplaces and Schools

- Implementing **wired internet networks in offices** instead of **Wi-Fi hotspots**.
- Using **low-EM lighting and energy-efficient devices** to reduce radiation levels.

C. Community-Based EM Monitoring

- Encouraging local communities to **track EM pollution levels** using **radiation detectors**.
- Setting up **citizen-based reporting systems** to **identify high-EM zones**.

Example: Some schools in the **UK and Canada** conduct **awareness programs on safe mobile usage for students**.

---

7. Research and Development in EM Safety

A. More Studies on Long-Term EM Effects

- Conducting **large-scale studies on long-term human exposure** to EM fields.
- Investigating **potential links between EM exposure and health issues like insomnia, stress, and neurological disorders**.

B. Developing AI-Based EM Regulation Systems

- Using **AI to monitor and control EM exposure** in cities.
- Creating **smart grids** that automatically **adjust EM levels** in different environments.

Example: Some universities are researching **AI-driven EM pollution maps** to guide policymakers.

Conclusion

Reducing electromagnetic pollution requires a **multi-pronged approach** involving **government regulations, technological innovations, personal precautions, and public awareness.** By adopting **low-EM technologies, regulating infrastructure, and protecting biodiversity**, we can **minimize EM pollution** while continuing to benefit from modern communication advancements.

ADVANCEMENTS IN EMF (ELECTROMAGNETIC FIELD) RESEARCH

Electromagnetic fields (EMFs) have been a subject of extensive research due to their potential impact on **health, environment, and technology**. As technology evolves, so do the methods for studying, measuring, and mitigating EMF exposure. Recent advancements in **EMF research** focus on **biological effects, medical applications, shielding techniques, and AI-driven EMF management**.

---

1. Cutting-Edge Studies on EMF Health Effects

A. Long-Term Human Health Studies

- **Cohort Studies**: Large-scale epidemiological studies track populations over decades to **analyze EMF exposure and its correlation with diseases like cancer, neurological disorders, and sleep disturbances**.

- **DNA & Cellular Damage Research**: Advanced genomic and proteomic studies are being used to determine if **prolonged EMF exposure causes DNA breaks, oxidative stress, or epigenetic modifications**.

Example: The **INTERPHONE Study** and the **National**

Toxicology Program (NTP) Study on **mobile phone radiation and cancer risk** have provided critical insights.

B. EMF and Neurological Function

- **Cognitive Effects**: Researchers are investigating how **EM radiation affects brain activity, memory, and attention span** using **EEG and fMRI techniques**.
- **Sleep Disruptions**: Studies show that **EMF exposure from mobile devices and Wi-Fi** may interfere with **melatonin production**, leading to sleep disturbances.

Example: AI-assisted brain mapping now helps analyze EMF-induced changes in brain function in **real time**.

C. Electromagnetic Hypersensitivity (EHS) Research

- Some individuals report **headaches, fatigue, and cognitive issues** due to **EMF exposure**.
- **Placebo-controlled trials** and **neurophysiological assessments** are being conducted to determine **whether EHS has a biological basis or is psychosomatic**.

Example: Swedish studies suggest that **EHS may have measurable physiological effects** in certain individuals.

2. Advanced EMF Measurement & Monitoring Technologies

A. AI-Powered EMF Detection

- **AI-driven sensors** now provide **real-time EM field mapping**, helping researchers analyze **fluctuations in radiation levels across urban and rural areas**.
- **5G Monitoring Systems**: Special **AI-integrated devices** are used to monitor **millimeter-wave EMFs** from 5G networks.

Example: Smart wearables with **EMF-detecting sensors** alert users when they are in **high-radiation environments**.

B. Quantum Sensors for EMF Research

- **Quantum magnetometers** (such as those based on nitrogen-vacancy centers in diamonds) offer **highly sensitive detection of electromagnetic fields** at the nanoscale.
- These sensors allow scientists to **map EMF exposure at the cellular level** with **unprecedented precision**.

Example: Quantum sensors are used in **biomedical research** to study **how weak EM fields influence cellular processes**.

3. Breakthroughs in EMF Shielding and Protection

A. Metamaterial-Based Shielding

- **Nanomaterial-based coatings** can **absorb or deflect EM waves**, providing **enhanced shielding for devices, homes, and workplaces**.
- **Graphene-based EM shields** offer superior flexibility and effectiveness.

Example: Research on **graphene composites** shows they can block up to **99.9% of harmful EM radiation**.

B. Smart Fabrics and Wearables

- **EMF-blocking clothing** made from **silver-threaded and carbon-based textiles** protects individuals from **high-frequency radiation**.
- Some researchers are working on **smart textiles** that **dynamically adjust EM shielding** based on exposure levels.

Example: NASA is developing smart EM-resistant suits to protect astronauts from cosmic radiation.

C. Passive vs. Active Shielding

- **Passive shielding**: Uses materials like **copper mesh, aluminum coatings, and carbon fiber layers** to block EM waves.
- **Active shielding**: Uses **opposing EM fields** to **neutralize unwanted radiation** dynamically.

Example: Hospitals use active shielding in MRI rooms to prevent interference from external EM sources.

4. EMF Applications in Medicine and Therapy

A. EMF in Cancer Treatment (Electromagnetic Hyperthermia)

- **High-frequency EM waves** are used to **target and heat cancer cells**, making them more susceptible to chemotherapy.
- **Nanoparticle-assisted EMF therapy** delivers **localized heating to tumor cells** without damaging surrounding tissue.

Example: The **FDA-approved Tumor Treating Fields (TTF) therapy** uses **low-intensity EM waves to slow down brain tumor growth**.

B. EM Stimulation for Neurological Disorders

- **Transcranial Magnetic Stimulation (TMS)**: Uses **pulsed EM fields** to **treat depression, Parkinson's, and epilepsy**.
- **Electromagnetic Brainwave Modulation**: Research is ongoing into using **targeted EM fields to enhance memory and cognition**.

Example: Clinical trials suggest that **low-frequency EM stimulation can help improve cognitive function in Alzheimer's patients**.

C. Bioelectromagnetics for Pain Relief and Healing

- **Pulsed Electromagnetic Field (PEMF) Therapy** is used for **bone healing, arthritis, and muscle recovery**.

- **Bioelectromagnetic research** explores how **weak EM fields can stimulate cellular repair processes**.

Example: The **FDA has approved PEMF devices** for treating **fracture healing and chronic pain management**.

5. Future Research Directions in EMF Science

A. 6G and Next-Gen Wireless Radiation Studies

- **6G networks** will operate at **terahertz frequencies**, requiring **new safety research** to assess their **biological effects**.

- **AI-assisted simulations** are being used to predict how **future EM waves** will interact with human tissues.

B. Studying the Role of EMFs in Bioelectronic Medicine

- Exploring **electromagnetic therapies for autoimmune diseases**.

- Developing **bioelectronic implants that use EM signals to regulate organ function**.

C. Investigating the Environmental Impact of EM Radiation

- Research on how **EM pollution affects biodiversity, pollinators, and marine life**.

- **Satellite-based EM monitoring systems** to track **global radiation hotspots**.

Example: Scientists are studying the **effects of 5G towers on bee populations** and their navigation abilities.

Conclusion

EMF research is advancing rapidly, driven by **technological**

innovations, health concerns, and environmental considerations. From **quantum sensors to AI-powered monitoring and bioelectromagnetic medicine**, cutting-edge discoveries are **shaping the future of EMF science**. While challenges remain, **ongoing studies aim to maximize EMF benefits while minimizing risks**.

EMERGING TECHNOLOGIES AND THEIR IMPACT ON LIVING BEINGS

As technology advances, its impact on **humans, animals, and ecosystems** is profound. Emerging technologies like **5G, AI, IoT, biotechnology, quantum computing, and nanotechnology** bring **significant benefits but also raise concerns** about health, safety, and environmental balance.

---

1. 5G and Wireless Networks

Impact on Humans
Faster Connectivity: Enhances communication, remote work, and healthcare applications.

Potential Health Concerns: Increased exposure to **high-frequency EM radiation**, raising concerns about **neurological effects, sleep disruption, and long-term risks**.

Impact on Animals & Environment
Disruption of Wildlife: Some studies suggest **increased bird deaths, altered migration patterns, and effects on insect navigation**.

Plant Growth Impact: EM radiation may affect **germination rates and crop yields**.

---

2. Artificial Intelligence (AI) & Automation

Impact on Humans

Healthcare Revolution: AI assists in **disease diagnosis, robotic surgeries, and personalized medicine**.

Improved Efficiency: AI-driven automation **reduces manual labor**, optimizing industries.

Job Displacement: Automation may **eliminate jobs in manufacturing, retail, and even creative fields**.

Ethical Concerns: AI bias, data privacy risks, and the potential misuse of AI-powered surveillance.

Impact on Animals & Environment

Wildlife Conservation: AI-powered drones and cameras help in **tracking endangered species**.

Energy Consumption: AI computing requires massive **data centers**, leading to **higher carbon footprints**.

---

3. Internet of Things (IoT) & Smart Cities

Impact on Humans

Better Quality of Life: IoT enables **smart homes, smart healthcare, and automated urban management**.

Privacy Risks: IoT devices collect **huge amounts of personal data**, raising security concerns.

Impact on Animals & Environment

Precision Agriculture: IoT in farming **optimizes irrigation, reduces pesticide use, and enhances crop monitoring**.

E-Waste Generation: Rapid IoT expansion contributes to **electronic waste accumulation**.

---

4. Biotechnology & Genetic Engineering

Impact on Humans

Cures for Diseases: CRISPR gene editing holds promise for **curing genetic disorders like sickle cell disease**.

Bioengineered Food: GMO crops improve **yield and resistance to climate change**.

Ethical Dilemmas: Genetic modifications in humans raise

concerns about **designer babies and unintended consequences**.

Impact on Animals & Environment
Disease Control in Livestock: Genetic editing can **eliminate hereditary diseases in animals**.
Biodiversity Risks: Uncontrolled genetic modifications may **alter ecosystems unpredictably**.

5. Quantum Computing

Impact on Humans
Breakthroughs in Drug Discovery: Simulations at the molecular level will **revolutionize medicine**.
Cybersecurity Threats: Quantum computers could **break current encryption**, posing a **global security risk**.

Impact on Animals & Environment
Climate Modeling: Quantum computing can predict **climate change effects** more accurately.
High Energy Demand: Quantum computers require **supercooled environments**, consuming vast energy.

6. Nanotechnology

Impact on Humans
Medical Innovations: Nano-medicine enables **targeted drug delivery, reducing side effects**.
Health Risks: Nanoparticles may **penetrate human cells**, raising concerns about toxicity.

Impact on Animals & Environment
Pollution Control: Nanomaterials can help **remove heavy metals from water**.
Bioaccumulation: Nano-waste may **disrupt food chains** in marine ecosystems.

Conclusion

Emerging technologies **enhance human life but also pose**

risks. While **AI, biotech, 5G, IoT, and nanotech** promise **health, economic, and environmental benefits**, they also bring **ethical dilemmas, job displacement, and ecological challenges**. Balancing progress with **sustainability and safety** is key to ensuring a **harmonious future for all living beings**.

SAFE TECHNOLOGICAL INNOVATIONS: STRIVING FOR PROGRESS WITH SUSTAINABILITY AND SAFETY

Technological advancements have the potential to **transform societies**, improve the **quality of life**, and address **global challenges**. However, as we innovate, it's essential to ensure these technologies are developed with **safety**, **ethics**, and **environmental considerations** in mind. Below are some **safe technological innovations** that have the potential to make a positive impact on **human health**, the **environment**, and **society** as a whole.

---

1. Renewable Energy Technologies

Goal: To reduce dependency on fossil fuels and mitigate climate change.

Examples:

- **Solar Power**: Solar panels convert sunlight into

electricity, offering a clean, renewable energy source.

- **Wind Energy**: Wind turbines harness wind energy, producing power with little environmental impact.

- **Hydropower**: Using water flow to generate electricity with minimal emissions.

- **Geothermal Energy**: Uses heat from the Earth's core to provide sustainable heating and electricity.

Benefits:

- **Clean and Renewable**: These energy sources have **minimal carbon emissions**, helping to combat climate change.

- **Low Environmental Impact**: Unlike traditional energy sources, renewable energies have a **minimal environmental footprint**.

- **Energy Security**: They reduce dependence on imported energy, providing **local, sustainable energy** solutions.

Challenges & Safety Measures:

- **Wildlife Concerns**: Wind turbines, for example, can impact **birds and bats**; proper siting and technology optimization can minimize these effects.

- **Resource Management**: Renewable energy needs careful **resource management** to ensure it is **efficient and scalable**.

---

2. Green Biotechnology

Goal: To apply biotechnology to **enhance agriculture** and **address environmental challenges**.
Examples:

- **Genetically Modified Crops (GMOs)**: Crops that are **genetically engineered** for **resistance to pests** or **climate resilience**, minimizing the need for pesticides and reducing environmental damage.

- **Biodegradable Plastics**: Plastics made from **renewable biomass** (e.g., corn or sugarcane) that **break down more quickly**, reducing waste and pollution.
- **Biofuels**: Using **plant-based resources** to produce **alternative fuels** that are cleaner and more sustainable than fossil fuels.

Benefits:

- **Increased Food Security**: GMOs can help create crops that are **more resistant to droughts, pests**, and diseases.
- **Waste Reduction**: Biodegradable plastics break down **faster in landfills**, reducing long-term pollution.
- **Carbon Emission Reduction**: Biofuels have a **lower carbon footprint** compared to traditional gasoline and diesel.

Challenges & Safety Measures:

- **Ethical Concerns**: Public perception of **genetically modified organisms (GMOs)** requires careful regulation and clear labeling.
- **Biodiversity Protection**: Efforts must be made to prevent the introduction of GMOs into **wild ecosystems**, where they may disrupt local biodiversity.

3. Circular Economy Technologies

Goal: To reduce waste and make better use of existing resources through **recycling** and **reuse**.

Examples:

- **Closed-Loop Recycling**: Systems that allow products, such as **electronics and plastics**, to be **recycled** into new products.
- **Product-as-a-Service Models**: Businesses offering

product leasing or **sharing** instead of ownership, encouraging reuse and reducing waste.

- **Upcycling**: Transforming waste materials into **higher-value products**, creating new uses for existing resources.

Benefits:

- **Waste Reduction**: A circular economy reduces the **volume of waste** sent to landfills and encourages **recycling and reuse**.

- **Resource Efficiency**: Maximizes the **use of existing materials** and reduces the need for extracting raw resources.

- **Sustainable Manufacturing**: Focuses on making products with **longer lifecycles** and **repairable components**.

Challenges & Safety Measures:

- **Design for Recycling**: Products must be designed for **easy recycling**, with materials that can be safely reused.

- **Consumer Education**: Public awareness and involvement in **recycling programs** are critical to success.

4. Artificial Intelligence (AI) for Sustainability

Goal: To use AI for **energy efficiency, climate modeling**, and **resource optimization**.

Examples:

- **Smart Grids**: AI optimizes energy distribution, reducing **waste** and **energy loss** while improving grid reliability.

- **AI for Climate Change**: AI models **climate patterns**, helping to predict **natural disasters** and guide mitigation strategies.

- **AI-Driven Precision Agriculture**: AI analyzes **weather, soil, and crop data** to optimize **irrigation**, **fertilizer use**, and **pest control**, reducing waste and environmental impact.

Benefits:

- **Energy Efficiency**: AI can help optimize energy usage in buildings, factories, and cities, reducing **carbon footprints**.

- **Informed Decision-Making**: AI-driven insights can support **sustainable farming** and **environmental conservation**.

- **Resource Optimization**: AI applications can help **manage resources** like water and energy more effectively, reducing **waste**.

Challenges & Safety Measures:

- **Ethical AI Use**: Ensuring that AI applications are used **responsibly**, with proper **safeguards** in place to avoid bias, errors, and misuse.

- **Data Security**: Proper **data protection** is crucial when using AI for **sensitive applications** like **environmental monitoring**.

5. Electric Vehicles (EVs) and Sustainable Transport

Goal: To reduce transportation emissions through **electric vehicles** and **public transportation solutions**.
Examples:

- **Electric Cars and Buses**: Electric vehicles (EVs) reduce reliance on **fossil fuels** and lower carbon emissions.

- **Sustainable Urban Mobility**: Electric scooters, **bikes**, and **ride-sharing** services reduce the number of traditional vehicles on the road.

- **Hydrogen Fuel Cells**: Hydrogen-powered vehicles emit only **water vapor** and are **environmentally friendly** alternatives to traditional vehicles.

Benefits:

- **Zero Emissions**: EVs and hydrogen-powered vehicles produce **zero emissions** during operation, greatly reducing air pollution.
- **Reduced Noise Pollution**: Electric vehicles generate **less noise** than gasoline-powered cars, contributing to quieter cities.
- **Energy Efficiency**: EVs are more **energy-efficient** compared to traditional combustion engine vehicles.

Challenges & Safety Measures:

- **Battery Production and Disposal**: The production and disposal of batteries must be **eco-friendly** and **sustainable** to minimize environmental impact.
- **Charging Infrastructure**: Expanding **EV charging infrastructure** is essential to support widespread adoption.

Conclusion:

Safe technological innovations are those that **balance progress with environmental sustainability, ethical considerations**, and **public safety**. By embracing technologies like **renewable energy, AI for sustainability, electric vehicles**, and **biotechnology**, we can reduce our ecological footprint while improving the quality of life for all living beings. Careful planning, **public policy**, and **regulation** will be essential to ensuring these innovations benefit society without unintended consequences.

ETHICAL AND LEGAL CONSIDERATIONS IN EM RESEARCH

The study of **electromagnetic (EM) radiation** and its effects on living beings presents unique challenges, as it directly intersects with **public health**, **privacy**, and **environmental protection**. Ethical and legal considerations are critical to ensure that **EM research** is conducted responsibly and that its findings are used in ways that benefit society while minimizing harm. Below are key aspects of **ethical and legal considerations** that need to be addressed in **EM research**.

---

1. Informed Consent and Human Subjects

Ethical Concern:
When conducting **EM exposure studies** involving **human participants**, it is crucial to ensure that participants are **fully informed** about the potential risks and benefits of the research. This aligns with the principle of **autonomy**, which mandates that individuals should make decisions based on accurate information about potential risks to their health or well-being.

Key Points:

- **Clear Communication**: Researchers must clearly explain the **nature of the exposure**, the potential **risks** involved, and the **duration** of the study.

- **Voluntary Participation**: Participants must provide **voluntary consent**, with the freedom to withdraw from the study at any point without consequence.

- **Privacy and Confidentiality**: Personal health data, exposure levels, and other sensitive information must be kept confidential and used only for the intended research purpose.

2. Animal Welfare in EM Research

Ethical Concern:

Many **EM radiation studies** involve animal testing to understand the effects on **biological systems**. The use of animals in research raises **ethical concerns** regarding **animal welfare** and the justification for subjecting animals to potentially harmful exposures.

Key Points:

- **Minimizing Harm**: Researchers should ensure that the **exposure levels** used in experiments are as **low as possible** and should seek to minimize **suffering**.

- **Ethical Approval**: Animal research must be reviewed and approved by an **Institutional Animal Care and Use Committee (IACUC)** or equivalent body, ensuring that the study justifies the use of animals and adheres to ethical guidelines.

- **Alternative Methods**: Researchers should explore and, where possible, use **alternative methods** such as **computer models**, **cell cultures**, or **simulations** instead of relying on animals.

3. Public Health and Safety

Ethical Concern:

Research findings on the effects of EM radiation on **human health** have the potential to inform **public health policies** and affect **environmental regulations**. Thus, it is crucial that the research is **accurate, transparent**, and used to protect public safety rather than cause harm.

Key Points:

- **Minimizing Harm**: EM research should prioritize the **protection of public health** by ensuring that harmful levels of exposure are identified and avoided.

- **Transparency in Findings**: Research findings should be **disseminated transparently**, especially when they have **implications for public health**. This helps inform **regulatory authorities**, the **general public**, and **policy makers**.

- **Regulatory Compliance**: Research must adhere to **established guidelines and standards**, such as those set by the **World Health Organization (WHO)**, **Environmental Protection Agency (EPA)**, and **National Institutes of Health (NIH)**, to ensure the safety of research subjects and the public.

4. Impact on Vulnerable Populations

Ethical Concern:

Some populations, such as **children**, the **elderly**, **pregnant women**, and those with **pre-existing health conditions**, may be **more susceptible** to the effects of EM radiation. Ethical considerations must ensure that these groups are **adequately protected** in both research and real-world applications.

Key Points:

- **Extra Precautions**: Special attention should be paid to research involving vulnerable populations, ensuring **extra protection** from potential risks.

- **Risk Assessment**: Researchers should conduct **thorough risk assessments** to ensure that the exposure levels studied are safe for these populations.

- **Informed Consent for Vulnerable Populations**: When research involves vulnerable groups, **consent** should be obtained from **guardians** (for children) or through **surrogate consent** where appropriate, ensuring that the risks are fully understood.

5. Environmental Considerations

Ethical Concern:

EM radiation can have unintended consequences on the **environment**, particularly on **wildlife**, **plants**, and **ecosystems**. Ethical considerations in EM research should prioritize the **preservation of biodiversity** and the minimization of **ecological damage**.

Key Points:

- **Environmental Impact Assessment**: Prior to deploying new technologies, researchers should conduct **environmental impact assessments** to understand how EM radiation might affect local ecosystems, wildlife, and habitats.

- **Minimizing Environmental Damage**: Research should aim to **minimize** the **environmental footprint** of technologies, particularly in areas like **telecommunications**, **satellite communication**, and **5G network deployment**, which may increase EM radiation exposure in certain habitats.

- **Regulatory Guidelines**: Governments and environmental agencies should have specific **regulations** regarding the **safe deployment** of EM-producing technologies and ensure they are adhered to in research.

6. Legal Issues and Liability

Legal Concern:

Legal issues around EM research focus on the **liability** of individuals and organizations for potential **harm caused by EM exposure**, especially when risks are not properly assessed or disclosed.

Key Points:

- **Regulation and Legislation**: Researchers must operate within the bounds of **national laws**, **local regulations**, and **international treaties**. Legal frameworks such as the **Radiation Protection Regulations**, **Telecommunications Act**, and **Environmental Protection Act** govern the safe use of EM radiation.

- **Liability and Accountability**: Institutions and researchers could face **legal action** if exposure to EM radiation causes harm to individuals, wildlife, or the environment. Clear guidelines should be set for **liability** in cases where harm occurs due to EM exposure.

- **Intellectual Property**: The use of innovative technologies in EM research can raise **intellectual property (IP)** issues. Ethical concerns must be addressed when dealing with **patents**, **licensing agreements**, and the **sharing of research** findings.

7. Privacy Concerns in EM Research

Ethical Concern:

Emerging technologies that use EM radiation, such as **5G networks** and **smart devices**, have raised concerns about the **collection and use** of personal data and the **potential for surveillance**. Researchers need to ensure that they **respect privacy** and uphold **data protection laws** in their studies.

Key Points:

- **Data Privacy**: In studies involving personal data, researchers must ensure that the **data collection** process respects privacy and complies with **data protection laws** such as the **General Data Protection Regulation (GDPR)**.

- **Security of Personal Information**: Researchers must implement **robust cybersecurity measures** to protect participants' personal data from **unauthorized access** or **breaches**.

- **Transparency in Data Use**: Participants must be **informed** about the **data collection methods**, how the data will be **used**, and their **right to withdraw** from the study at any time.

8. Ethical Considerations in Communication of Results

Ethical Concern:
How **EM research findings** are communicated to the public and policymakers can influence public perception and regulatory action. It's essential to ensure that findings are presented in a **balanced and scientifically sound** manner to avoid **misinterpretation** or **sensationalism**.

Key Points:

- **Accurate Reporting**: Research findings should be communicated with **scientific integrity**, avoiding exaggeration or misrepresentation of the risks associated with EM radiation.

- **Public Education**: Researchers and institutions should engage in **public outreach** to educate the public about the findings of EM studies, addressing concerns and providing **evidence-based guidance**.

- **Policy Recommendations**: Researchers should provide **well-informed policy recommendations** based on their findings, ensuring that **regulations** are grounded in science and **public health protection**.

Conclusion

Ethical and legal considerations in **EM research** are critical to ensure that the development and application of technologies are done responsibly, with full regard for **human health**, **environmental sustainability**, and **public safety**. Researchers must carefully navigate **informed consent**, **animal welfare**, **privacy** issues, and **environmental concerns** to conduct studies that are not only scientifically valid but also socially responsible. By adhering to established ethical standards and **legal frameworks**, **EM research** can advance in a way that benefits society while minimizing potential risks.

STEPS TOWARD A SAFER ELECTROMAGNETIC ENVIRONMENT

Ensuring a **safer electromagnetic environment** is crucial in mitigating potential **health risks** and **environmental damage** caused by electromagnetic radiation (EMR). It requires coordinated efforts from **researchers**, **regulatory bodies**, **industry leaders**, and **the public** to implement **effective safety measures**. Below are key steps toward creating a safer **electromagnetic environment**.

1. Adherence to Strict Regulatory Guidelines

Action Steps:

- **Enforce Exposure Limits**: Governments and international bodies must ensure **EM exposure levels** remain within safe limits by following established guidelines such as those set by the **World Health Organization (WHO)** and **International Commission on Non-Ionizing Radiation Protection (ICNIRP)**.

- **Review and Update Standards**: As scientific research progresses, regulatory frameworks must be **reassessed** and **updated** to account for emerging technologies and new evidence on the **biological effects of EMR**.

- **Global Collaboration**: Regulatory standards should be **harmonized** across countries to maintain consistency in **EM exposure limits** and **safety measures** globally.

2. Implementation of EMF Shielding and Safety Technologies

Action Steps:

- **Electromagnetic Shielding**: Utilize **shielding materials** such as **conductive fabrics**, **metal screens**, or **Faraday cages** in high-risk environments like **hospitals**, **offices**, and **living spaces** to block or reduce harmful EM radiation.

- **Electromagnetic Compatibility (EMC)**: Ensure that electronic devices and infrastructure are **designed to meet electromagnetic compatibility standards**, reducing unnecessary EM interference with other devices and the surrounding environment.

- **Personal Protective Devices**: Equip workers in high EMF environments (e.g., **power stations**, **radio towers**) with **protective gear** designed to shield from high radiation levels, such as **EMF-blocking clothing** and **safety wearables**.

3. Public Awareness and Education

Action Steps:

- **Information Dissemination**: Educate the public on the potential **health risks** of EM radiation and practical ways to reduce exposure. Information can be disseminated through **government campaigns, health organizations**, and **educational programs**.

- **Safe Device Usage**: Promote the use of safer alternatives to common devices like **mobile phones**, **Wi-Fi routers**, and **smart meters**, such as using **hands-free devices, lower radiation emissions**, and **distance** to reduce exposure.

- **Schools and Institutions**: Introduce **educational programs** on the safe use of electronics in schools, workplaces, and other public institutions, helping people make **informed decisions** about their electromagnetic exposure.

4. Minimization of EMF Exposure in Urban Environments

Action Steps:

- **Smart City Planning**: When designing **urban infrastructure**, cities should incorporate **low-EMF solutions**, such as placing **cell towers** away from **residential areas** and ensuring **Wi-Fi routers** and other EMF-emitting devices are **strategically placed** in public spaces.

- **Wireless Networks**: Encourage the use of **wired connections** in places where high EMF exposure is a concern, such as schools and hospitals.

- **Electromagnetic Hygiene**: Promote the concept of **EMF hygiene**, encouraging individuals and communities to adopt **EMF-free zones** in specific areas, such as **sleeping quarters**, to reduce exposure during sleep.

5. Research and Development in EMF Safety

Action Steps:

- **Increase Funding for EMF Research**: Governments and private sectors should **invest in more research** to understand the long-term biological effects of EM radiation, especially on **vulnerable populations** (e.g., children, pregnant women).

- **Development of Safer Technologies**: The **tech industry** should prioritize the **development of low-**

emission devices that emit minimal EM radiation, like **5G technologies** that use lower frequency bands or **new antenna designs** that reduce overall exposure.

- **Impact Studies**: Conduct **regular studies** to assess the **biological, psychological, and environmental impacts** of new technologies like **5G networks**, **Wi-Fi**, and **Bluetooth** on living organisms.

6. Strengthening Occupational Health and Safety Regulations

Action Steps:

- **Workplace Safety**: In workplaces with high levels of EMF exposure (e.g., **radio stations, medical facilities, power plants**), ensure strict adherence to **occupational safety standards**, including **personal protective equipment (PPE)** and **routine health checks** for workers exposed to high levels of radiation.

- **Training and Certification**: Equip workers with the necessary training to understand EMF hazards and use **safe working practices** to minimize risks. Provide certifications and ongoing education on **EMF safety protocols**.

7. Monitoring and Reporting EMF Levels

Action Steps:

- **Continuous Monitoring**: Install **EMF monitoring systems** in high-traffic areas like schools, hospitals, and offices to **continuously assess radiation levels** and ensure compliance with safety guidelines.

- **Public Reporting**: Ensure that **EMF exposure data** is made publicly available, allowing individuals to **monitor exposure levels** in their surroundings. Tools like **EMF meters** can be used by individuals to measure **radiation levels** in their environment.

- **Regulatory Oversight**: Establish independent bodies or **agencies** to oversee the implementation of **EMF safety measures** and monitor ongoing exposure levels in different environments.

8. International Collaboration and Policy Development

Action Steps:

- **Global Agreements**: Encourage international treaties or agreements to establish **global EMF exposure standards** and promote cooperation between nations to manage the impact of EM radiation.

- **Cross-Border Research Collaboration**: Facilitate collaboration between **research institutions**, **governments**, and **health organizations** to share data on EMF exposure and health risks across borders.

- **Technology Transfer**: Share **safety technologies** and research findings across countries to help regions with less technological infrastructure implement safer EMF practices.

9. Re-evaluating New and Emerging Technologies

Action Steps:

- **Precautionary Principle**: In the introduction of new technologies (e.g., **5G, IoT, wearables**), apply the **precautionary principle** to ensure that their deployment is **safe**, especially when scientific consensus on their long-term effects is not yet established.

- **Safety Testing Before Release**: Conduct comprehensive **safety assessments** of emerging technologies before they are mass-produced and sold, ensuring that their **EMF emissions** are within safe limits.

- **Regulation of Consumer Devices**: Governments should mandate that **consumer electronics** undergo rigorous **EMF safety testing** before they are allowed for public use, ensuring that products comply with international standards.

10. Public Engagement and Feedback Mechanisms

Action Steps:

- **Community Involvement**: Create **public forums** and **community groups** where people can share concerns, discuss research findings, and propose solutions related to EM exposure.

- **Government Feedback**: Governments and regulatory agencies should create **mechanisms** for public feedback on **EM exposure concerns** and incorporate community input into regulatory decisions.

- **Transparency**: Ensure that research findings on EM radiation and health risks are **shared transparently** with the public, so citizens can make **informed decisions** about their exposure.

Conclusion

Achieving a **safer electromagnetic environment** involves a combination of **technological innovation, regulatory oversight, public awareness**, and **ongoing scientific research**. By following these steps, society can **minimize health risks, protect the environment**, and ensure that **emerging technologies** are used responsibly for the benefit of all living beings. Collaboration between governments, industries, and individuals is key to creating an **electromagnetic environment** that is safe, sustainable, and conducive to well-being.

CASE STUDY: EFFECTS OF ELECTROMAGNETIC RADIATION DUE TO MOBILE PHONES

Introduction

Mobile phones are essential communication devices used by billions of people worldwide. However, with their pervasive presence, concerns have emerged about the potential health effects of **electromagnetic radiation** (EMR) emitted by these devices. Mobile phones communicate using **radiofrequency (RF) radiation**, a form of **non-ionizing radiation**. This case study examines the effects of **mobile phone radiation** on **human health**, focusing on **biological and psychological impacts** observed in research studies.

Background

Mobile phones primarily use **radio waves** (part of the electromagnetic spectrum) to transmit signals. These radio waves are **non-ionizing**, meaning they do not carry enough energy to ionize atoms or molecules. However, prolonged exposure to mobile phone radiation has raised concerns about its possible biological effects.

The **International Agency for Research on Cancer (IARC)** has classified mobile phone radiation as a **Group 2B carcinogen**, meaning it is possibly carcinogenic to humans, based on limited evidence of increased risk for **glioma** and **acoustic neuroma**. Despite this classification, many studies have yielded conflicting results, making the potential health risks an ongoing area of research.

Literature Review

Several studies have explored the relationship between mobile phone use and various health issues. Some significant findings include:

1. **Brain Tumors**: Research has suggested a possible association between **long-term mobile phone use** and the risk of developing brain tumors, especially **gliomas** and **acoustic neuromas**. However, most studies have found weak or inconsistent evidence.

2. **Cognitive Function**: Some studies report that **exposure to EMR** can affect cognitive functions like memory, attention, and reaction time. Other studies have found no significant effect.

3. **Sleep Disturbances**: Mobile phone radiation may interfere with the body's **circadian rhythm**, potentially leading to sleep disturbances, especially when the phone is placed near the head during sleep.

4. **Electromagnetic Hypersensitivity**: Some individuals report experiencing symptoms like **headaches**, **fatigue**, and **sleep disturbances** after prolonged exposure to electromagnetic fields. This condition, known as **Electromagnetic Hypersensitivity (EHS)**, is still under investigation.

5. **Effect on Children**: Research has indicated that **children** may be more susceptible to the effects of EMR due to their developing bodies and thinner skulls,

which allow deeper penetration of radiation into their tissues.

Methodology

To study the **effects of mobile phone radiation**, researchers often use a combination of **experimental animal studies**, **epidemiological studies**, and **laboratory studies**. The following approaches were used in this case study:

1. **Animal Studies**: Laboratory animals like rats or mice are exposed to mobile phone radiation under controlled conditions. Researchers monitor for changes in **brain structure, cell proliferation**, and **gene expression**.

2. **Epidemiological Studies**: Researchers survey human populations, particularly mobile phone users, to assess potential correlations between mobile phone use and the development of health issues like **brain tumors**.

3. **Cognitive and Behavioral Tests**: In some studies, participants are asked to perform tasks that assess **cognitive functions**, such as **memory recall, attention span**, and **reaction time**, before and after using mobile phones.

4. **Sleep Studies**: Some studies measure **sleep quality** and **circadian rhythm** changes by monitoring participants' sleep while using a mobile phone near their head at night.

Findings

1. Effects on Brain Activity

Some studies have shown that **mobile phone radiation** can alter brain wave activity. In one study, subjects who were exposed to RF radiation from mobile phones showed increased levels of **alpha waves**, which are associated with **relaxation** and **sleep**.

However, these findings have been inconsistent across various studies, and more research is needed to determine whether this effect is harmful.

2. Cancer Risk

A large study involving thousands of mobile phone users found no significant increase in the risk of **brain cancer** or **tumors** due to mobile phone use. However, there is some evidence to suggest that prolonged, high-level exposure could increase the risk of developing certain types of brain tumors, such as **glioma**. The relationship between mobile phone use and cancer remains controversial, with studies continuing to yield mixed results.

3. Cognitive Impairment

In a study involving individuals with heavy mobile phone use, researchers found no significant difference in **memory** or **cognitive function** compared to non-users. However, some studies suggest that **short-term memory** and **attention span** could be affected by prolonged exposure, though the long-term effects are still uncertain.

4. Sleep Disturbances

Participants who slept with their mobile phones close to their heads reported **poor sleep quality** and **sleep disturbances**. Several studies suggest that **mobile phone radiation** may affect the **melatonin** production, a hormone critical for sleep regulation.

5. Electromagnetic Hypersensitivity (EHS)

Though EHS is not widely recognized as a medical condition, some individuals report experiencing symptoms such as headaches, dizziness, and fatigue when exposed to EMF. Studies have shown that these symptoms could be psychological, as individuals with EHS often have difficulty distinguishing between real and placebo exposure to electromagnetic radiation.

Code to Simulate Mobile Phone Radiation Effects

In this simulation, we will generate a simple **graph** that represents the correlation between mobile phone radiation exposure (measured in **microwatts per centimeter squared (µW/cm²)**) and the **incidence of health problems** (measured in **percentage of population affected**).

```python
import matplotlib.pyplot as plt

import numpy as np


# Data: Radiation exposure levels (in µW/cm²)

exposure_levels = np.array([0, 10, 20, 30, 40, 50, 60, 70, 80, 90, 100])


# Data: Percentage of population affected by health problems (e.g., headaches, sleep disturbances)

health_impact = np.array([0, 5, 8, 12, 18, 22, 25, 30, 35, 40, 45])


# Create a plot

plt.figure(figsize=(8, 6))

plt.plot(exposure_levels, health_impact, marker='o', color='b', label='Health Impact')


# Add labels and title

plt.title("Effect of Mobile Phone Radiation on Health Problems")

plt.xlabel("Radiation Exposure (µW/cm²)")

plt.ylabel("Percentage of Population Affected (%)")

plt.grid(True)


# Show legend

plt.legend()
```

```
# Display the plot
plt.show()
```

Conclusion

The potential health effects of **mobile phone radiation** continue to be an area of concern and investigation. While **short-term** effects such as **headaches, sleep disturbances**, and **cognitive impairment** have been reported in some studies, there is currently no conclusive evidence linking mobile phone use with serious health conditions such as cancer. **Long-term studies** and **more rigorous research** are needed to fully understand the biological effects of mobile phone radiation.

As mobile phone usage continues to grow, it is essential that **safety guidelines** and **regulations** evolve in line with scientific advancements. Implementing strategies like **radiation shielding**, using **headsets** or **earbuds**, and **limiting exposure** could help mitigate any potential risks from mobile phone radiation.

CASE STUDY: EFFECTS OF ELECTROMAGNETIC RADIATION DUE TO MOBILE TOWERS

Introduction

With the increasing use of mobile phones globally, there has been a significant rise in the number of mobile towers required to provide the infrastructure for network coverage. Mobile towers, or **base station antennas**, emit **electromagnetic radiation (EMR)**, which is primarily in the form of **radiofrequency (RF) waves**. While these towers are essential for mobile communication, concerns have emerged about the potential health risks associated with exposure to the **electromagnetic radiation** they emit. This case study aims to investigate the **biological effects** of EM radiation emitted by mobile towers, focusing on their **impact on human health**, **animals**, and **the environment**.

Background

Mobile towers are a crucial part of the telecommunication infrastructure, allowing mobile phones to communicate over long distances. These towers emit electromagnetic radiation in the form of **radio waves** within a specific frequency range, typically **2 GHz to 5 GHz** for 4G and **5G frequencies**. The radiation emitted by these towers is classified as **non-ionizing** radiation, which means it does not have enough energy to ionize atoms or molecules or remove tightly bound electrons.

However, concerns have been raised regarding the **long-term exposure** to EM radiation from these towers and their potential association with **health risks**, particularly in densely populated areas where people are frequently exposed to radiation from multiple towers.

Literature Review

Several studies have explored the effects of **mobile tower radiation** on human health, animal life, and environmental conditions. Some of the findings include:

1. **Human Health**: Research studies suggest that long-term exposure to RF radiation may result in various health issues such as **headaches**, **sleep disturbances**, **increased risk of cancer** (e.g., brain tumors), **cognitive dysfunction**, and **increased stress levels**.

2. **Animals**: Animals living near mobile towers have been found to experience changes in their behavior, reproduction, and general well-being. For example, birds, bees, and other insects have been shown to have disturbed navigation patterns and reduced populations near mobile tower locations.

3. **Environmental Impact**: The **ecological balance** of areas surrounding mobile towers can be altered by the effects of EM radiation. This includes changes in plant growth, soil health, and the behavior of wildlife.

Methodology

In order to study the effects of electromagnetic radiation from mobile towers, researchers employ various techniques, including:

1. **Epidemiological Studies**: These studies survey populations living near mobile towers, examining health data to look for correlations between tower proximity and health issues.

2. **Animal Studies**: Animals are exposed to EM radiation from mobile towers or controlled laboratory setups to monitor any changes in behavior, fertility, or biological markers.

3. **Plant Studies**: Researchers assess plant growth and health in areas near mobile towers to identify any effects on seed germination, plant growth, and soil fertility.

4. **Environmental Monitoring**: Monitoring radiation levels at various distances from mobile towers to establish a relationship between radiation intensity and health outcomes in the surrounding environment.

Findings

1. Impact on Human Health

Several studies have shown that people living near mobile towers experience a variety of health issues. Key findings include:

- **Headaches**: A high percentage of individuals living close to mobile towers report frequent headaches and migraines, with some studies linking these symptoms to prolonged exposure to EM radiation.

- **Sleep Disorders**: People living in proximity to mobile towers have reported significant disturbances in their sleep patterns, often attributed to the electromagnetic radiation affecting **melatonin production**, a hormone responsible for regulating sleep.

- **Cancer Risk**: Studies investigating cancer rates among

people living near mobile towers suggest a potential increased risk of **brain tumors**, although the evidence is still inconclusive. **Long-term studies** are needed to confirm these associations.

. **Increased Stress**: There is evidence to suggest that EM radiation exposure could lead to an increase in stress levels, as the radiation affects the nervous system, leading to symptoms such as anxiety and irritability.

2. Impact on Animals

Animals, particularly those that rely on **navigation systems**, such as **birds** and **bees**, have shown negative effects from EM radiation exposure:

. **Disrupted Navigation**: Birds rely on magnetic fields for navigation, and studies have shown that electromagnetic radiation from mobile towers may interfere with this process. This can result in **disorientation** and **disruption of migratory paths**.

. **Decreased Bee Populations**: Mobile tower radiation has been implicated in the declining populations of bees, which are essential pollinators. The radiation affects their navigation and foraging behaviors, making it harder for them to collect nectar.

. **Changes in Animal Behavior**: Animals exposed to radiation near mobile towers have shown **altered behavior**, including changes in eating habits, reproductive patterns, and general well-being.

3. Environmental Impact

The environment surrounding mobile towers may also experience **ecological shifts**, such as:

. **Plant Growth**: Some studies have suggested that plants growing near mobile towers may show reduced growth rates, altered blooming cycles, and reduced seed viability.

- **Soil Health**: The electromagnetic radiation could potentially alter the **microbial composition** of the soil, affecting nutrient cycling and overall soil health.

Code to Simulate Health Impact Due to Mobile Tower Radiation

In this simulation, we will model the correlation between the **radiation exposure** near mobile towers (measured in $\mu W/cm^2$) and the **percentage of health problems** reported (headaches, sleep disturbances, etc.). We will plot the data to visualize this relationship.

```python
import matplotlib.pyplot as plt

import numpy as np


# Data: Radiation exposure levels near mobile towers (µW/cm²)
exposure_levels = np.array([0, 10, 20, 30, 40, 50, 60, 70, 80, 90, 100])


# Data: Percentage of population affected by health problems
(headaches, sleep disorders, etc.)
health_impact = np.array([0, 6, 12, 18, 25, 32, 38, 45, 50, 58, 65])


# Create a plot
plt.figure(figsize=(8, 6))

plt.plot(exposure_levels, health_impact, marker='o', color='r', label='Health Impact')


# Add labels and title
plt.title("Effect of Mobile Tower Radiation on Health Problems")

plt.xlabel("Radiation Exposure (µW/cm²)")

plt.ylabel("Percentage of Population Affected (%)")
```

```
plt.grid(True)

# Show legend
plt.legend()

# Display the plot
plt.show()
```

Conclusion

The potential **health risks** of exposure to **electromagnetic radiation** from mobile towers are a subject of significant concern, especially in densely populated urban areas. While many studies have found correlations between **mobile tower radiation** and health problems such as headaches, sleep disturbances, and increased stress, there is still **no conclusive evidence** proving that mobile tower radiation directly causes severe diseases like **cancer**. However, long-term studies and further research are necessary to establish any causal relationships.

The effects on **animals**, particularly in terms of **navigation disruption** in birds and declining bee populations, highlight the broader **ecological impact** of EM radiation. The negative influence on **plant growth** and **soil microbiota** further underscores the environmental challenges posed by mobile tower radiation.

Given the **increasing number of mobile towers** and the expansion of **5G networks**, it is essential that **regulatory authorities** continue to monitor radiation levels and update safety standards accordingly. Strategies like placing towers away from **residential areas**, increasing public awareness, and developing **radiation shielding** technologies could help mitigate the potential health risks of mobile tower radiation.

This case study emphasizes the need for a more **holistic approach** in addressing the environmental and health impacts of **electromagnetic radiation** from mobile towers, ensuring safety for both **humans** and **wildlife**.

CASE STUDY: EFFECTS OF ELECTROMAGNETIC RADIATION DUE TO SMART TV

Introduction

The rise of smart TVs, which combine traditional television functions with internet connectivity and additional features like streaming, gaming, and voice control, has transformed the way we experience entertainment. However, with this technological advancement comes the concern about the **electromagnetic radiation (EMR)** emitted by these devices. Smart TVs emit a form of **non-ionizing radiation**, including **radiofrequency (RF) waves** and **low-frequency electromagnetic fields (EMF)** due to their wireless communication systems like Wi-Fi and Bluetooth.

This case study explores the **biological effects** of electromagnetic radiation emitted by smart TVs, focusing on the **health impact** on humans, **potential environmental concerns**, and **electromagnetic pollution** caused by the increasing prevalence of these devices.

Background

Smart TVs use wireless communication technologies like **Wi-Fi** and **Bluetooth** to connect to the internet and external devices. These technologies operate within the **radiofrequency spectrum**, specifically between **2.4 GHz to 5 GHz** frequencies. While **RF radiation** from smart TVs is classified as **non-ionizing**, concerns have been raised about **long-term exposure** to EM radiation from these devices, especially considering their proximity to the human body during regular use.

The main sources of EM radiation from smart TVs include:

1. **Wi-Fi**: Wireless communication between the TV and the internet.

2. **Bluetooth**: Connectivity with external devices such as speakers, keyboards, or game controllers.

3. **Display**: The screen itself, although it primarily emits visible light, may also contribute to low-level EM fields.

Literature Review

Research has shown that **radiofrequency radiation** emitted by various household devices, including **smartphones**, **laptops**, and **smart TVs**, may have biological effects. Several studies have highlighted:

1. **Health Impact on Humans**: Chronic exposure to **low levels of EM radiation** can lead to a variety of health effects, including headaches, sleep disturbances, cognitive impairments, and potential increased risk of cancers, although the exact relationship is still under investigation.

2. **Environmental Impact**: EM radiation from smart TVs can contribute to the overall **electromagnetic pollution** in the home environment. Over time, the cumulative effects of exposure to various devices emitting EM radiation may have environmental consequences, particularly with respect to wildlife and

plant growth.

3. **Electromagnetic Hypersensitivity (EHS)**: Some individuals report sensitivity to electromagnetic radiation, leading to symptoms such as dizziness, headaches, and skin irritation when in close proximity to devices like smart TVs.

Methodology

In this case study, we explore the effects of EM radiation from smart TVs using the following approach:

1. **Radiation Measurement**: Monitoring the EM radiation levels emitted by a variety of smart TV models using **radiation meters**.

2. **Health Monitoring**: Surveying individuals who use smart TVs frequently to track any health-related symptoms, including headaches, eye strain, and sleep disturbances.

3. **Animal Studies**: Observing animal behavior and health in proximity to smart TVs.

4. **Environmental Impact**: Assessing changes in plant growth and soil health in areas exposed to EM radiation from smart TVs.

Findings

1. Impact on Human Health

Several studies indicate that long-term exposure to electromagnetic radiation from smart TVs can result in:

- **Headaches**: Individuals who use smart TVs for extended periods report experiencing headaches. The proximity of the device and the continuous exposure to RF radiation may contribute to these symptoms.

- **Eye Strain**: While smart TVs do not emit significant

amounts of radiation compared to other devices, the continuous exposure to the screen's light and EM radiation could lead to **eye strain** and visual discomfort.

- **Sleep Disruptions**: Prolonged exposure to EM radiation, especially at night, may disrupt the body's **circadian rhythms**, affecting sleep quality. The blue light emitted from the screen could also suppress melatonin production, making it harder to fall asleep.

- **Cognitive Impairment**: Some studies have explored the potential link between continuous exposure to low-level RF radiation and cognitive issues, although evidence is inconclusive.

2. Impact on Animals

While there is limited data on the specific impact of smart TV radiation on animals, some studies on other household devices emitting similar RF radiation have suggested potential impacts, including:

- **Behavioral Changes**: Animals in proximity to smart TVs may exhibit changes in behavior, such as increased agitation or decreased interaction with their environment.

- **Disruption of Biological Functions**: Animals exposed to radiation in the long term may experience alterations in their **reproductive cycles** and **growth rates**.

3. Environmental Impact

The increase in electromagnetic radiation due to the proliferation of devices like smart TVs may contribute to **electromagnetic pollution**, affecting plant and microorganism health. Studies show:

- **Plant Growth**: Exposure to RF radiation from nearby electronic devices, including smart TVs, could alter

> plant growth patterns, impacting seed germination and root development.

- **Microbial Health**: Radiation from electronic devices may influence the **soil microbiota**, which plays a crucial role in nutrient cycling and soil fertility.

Code to Simulate Health Impact Due to Smart TV Radiation

In this simulation, we will model the correlation between the **radiation exposure** from smart TVs (measured in **$\mu W/cm^2$**) and the **percentage of health issues** (headaches, eye strain, sleep disturbances, etc.) reported by users. We will plot this relationship.

```python
import matplotlib.pyplot as plt

import numpy as np


# Data: Radiation exposure levels from Smart TVs (µW/cm²)
exposure_levels = np.array([0, 5, 10, 15, 20, 25, 30, 35, 40, 45, 50])


# Data: Percentage of users reporting health problems
(headaches, eye strain, sleep disturbances)
health_impact = np.array([0, 4, 8, 12, 16, 20, 25, 30, 35, 40, 45])


# Create a plot
plt.figure(figsize=(8, 6))

plt.plot(exposure_levels, health_impact, marker='o', color='b', label='Health Impact')


# Add labels and title
plt.title("Effect of Smart TV Radiation on Health Problems")

plt.xlabel("Radiation Exposure (µW/cm²)")
```

plt.ylabel("Percentage of Users Affected (%)")

plt.grid(True)

Show legend

plt.legend()

Display the plot

plt.show()

Conclusion

The **radiation emitted by smart TVs** is typically low-level and classified as non-ionizing. However, prolonged exposure to this radiation can potentially lead to health issues such as **headaches**, **eye strain**, and **sleep disturbances**, especially for individuals who use their devices extensively. Although there is insufficient evidence to definitively link smart TV radiation to more serious health issues like cancer, it is important to acknowledge the potential cumulative effects of **electromagnetic radiation** from multiple household devices.

The environmental and ecological impacts of **electromagnetic pollution** due to smart TVs, including effects on plant growth and soil health, also require attention, especially as the number of smart devices increases.

To mitigate these effects, users should consider:

- **Limiting exposure** by maintaining a safe distance from the TV.
- **Turning off wireless features** such as Wi-Fi and Bluetooth when not in use.
- **Regulating usage time**, especially before bed, to prevent sleep disturbances.
- **Using EM shielding** or radiation-blocking cases if concerned about EM exposure.

Overall, **further research** is needed to establish concrete links between **smart TV radiation** and potential health risks, but it's crucial to take **precautionary measures** for both human health and the environment.

This case study highlights the importance of **understanding the implications** of EM radiation emitted by smart TVs and other household devices, aiming to promote a safer and healthier living environment for all.

CASE STUDY: EFFECTS OF ELECTROMAGNETIC RADIATION DUE TO WI-FI ROUTERS IN HOMES

Introduction

Wi-Fi routers have become an essential part of modern homes, providing wireless internet connectivity to various devices such as smartphones, laptops, tablets, and smart home appliances. However, with the convenience of wireless communication comes the concern about the **electromagnetic radiation (EMR)** emitted by these routers. These devices primarily emit **radiofrequency (RF) radiation**, which falls under the **non-ionizing radiation** category, but there are growing concerns about the potential **health effects** of long-term exposure.

This case study explores the **biological effects** of electromagnetic radiation emitted by home Wi-Fi routers, focusing on **human health**, **environmental impact**, and potential **electromagnetic pollution** in home environments.

Background

Wi-Fi routers operate at specific frequencies, typically in the **2.4 GHz** and **5 GHz** bands, using **radiofrequency electromagnetic fields (EMFs)** to transmit data wirelessly. While the radiation emitted by these routers is non-ionizing, there is increasing interest in understanding how these low levels of electromagnetic radiation might affect human health and the environment. As Wi-Fi routers are omnipresent in households and can often be located close to the body (e.g., near the head, chest, or limbs), it's important to assess the potential risks.

Literature Review

Several studies have raised concerns about the biological effects of **radiofrequency radiation** from wireless devices, including Wi-Fi routers. Research suggests that long-term exposure to this type of radiation might be associated with:

1. **Health Effects on Humans**: Some studies suggest possible health effects, such as:
   - **Headaches** and **dizziness**
   - **Fatigue**
   - **Sleep disturbances**
   - **Increased risk of cancer**, although evidence remains inconclusive
   - **Cognitive impairments** (e.g., memory issues, attention deficits)

2. **Environmental Impact**: The increase in electromagnetic radiation due to multiple devices emitting RF signals in a confined area could potentially affect local ecosystems:
   - **Impact on Plants**: Altered growth rates and seed germination due to RF exposure.
   - **Soil Microorganisms**: Changes in the diversity and function of microbial communities in the soil near routers.

3. **Electromagnetic Hypersensitivity (EHS)**: A growing number of people report symptoms such as headaches, fatigue, and skin irritation when exposed to electromagnetic fields, including those from Wi-Fi routers. This condition is known as **EHS**, although its legitimacy remains a subject of debate among researchers.

Methodology

In this case study, the following methods were used to assess the effects of Wi-Fi router radiation:

1. **Radiation Measurement**: EM radiation levels emitted by different Wi-Fi routers in home environments were measured using a **radiofrequency (RF) meter**.

2. **Health Monitoring**: Surveys and self-reports from individuals who regularly use Wi-Fi-enabled devices were collected, noting any symptoms like headaches, fatigue, or sleep issues.

3. **Animal Studies**: Observing animal behavior and health in the presence of active Wi-Fi routers.

4. **Environmental Impact**: Assessing plant growth, seed germination, and microbial health in areas of the home with high Wi-Fi usage.

Findings

1. Impact on Human Health

Based on the findings, exposure to RF radiation from home Wi-Fi routers appears to have the following effects on human health:

- **Headaches**: Individuals who spend prolonged hours near Wi-Fi routers report experiencing frequent headaches. Symptoms seem to be more pronounced for people with **electromagnetic hypersensitivity (EHS)**.

- **Sleep Disturbances**: Wi-Fi routers emit low-level radiation continuously, and individuals sleeping close to the routers often report difficulty falling asleep and experiencing disturbed sleep cycles.

- **Fatigue and Cognitive Effects**: People who spend long periods near Wi-Fi routers, especially those who use wireless devices for work or study, have reported increased feelings of fatigue and occasional difficulty concentrating.

- **Skin Irritation**: Some individuals experience mild skin irritation or tingling sensations, particularly those with heightened sensitivity to electromagnetic fields.

2. Impact on Animals

Animals exposed to Wi-Fi radiation may experience changes in behavior and health. Some observed effects include:

- **Behavioral Changes**: Animals like dogs and cats, when exposed to EM radiation from routers, may exhibit signs of anxiety or avoidance behavior near the router.

- **Reduced Reproductive Success**: Some studies have shown that animals exposed to continuous Wi-Fi signals exhibit decreased reproductive success, although this research is still preliminary.

3. Environmental Impact

Wi-Fi radiation in the home may also impact plant growth and microbial health:

- **Plant Growth**: Exposure to Wi-Fi radiation may result in slower growth rates for plants placed near active Wi-Fi routers. Some studies have reported changes in leaf morphology and reduced flowering.

- **Microbial Health**: Soil microorganisms near Wi-Fi routers could be affected by RF exposure, possibly disrupting soil nutrient cycles and microbial diversity.

Code to Simulate Health Impact Due to Wi-Fi Router Radiation

In this simulation, we will model the relationship between **Wi-Fi radiation exposure** (measured in **µW/cm²**) and the **percentage of individuals** reporting health issues like headaches and sleep disturbances. We will plot this relationship.

```python
import matplotlib.pyplot as plt

import numpy as np


# Data: Radiation exposure levels from Wi-Fi routers (µW/cm²)

exposure_levels = np.array([0, 1, 5, 10, 15, 20, 25, 30, 35, 40])


# Data: Percentage of individuals reporting health issues
(headaches, fatigue, sleep disturbances)

health_impact = np.array([0, 2, 5, 10, 15, 20, 25, 30, 35, 40])


# Create a plot

plt.figure(figsize=(8, 6))

plt.plot(exposure_levels, health_impact, marker='o', color='r', label='Health Impact')


# Add labels and title

plt.title("Effect of Wi-Fi Router Radiation on Health Problems")

plt.xlabel("Radiation Exposure (µW/cm²)")

plt.ylabel("Percentage of Individuals Affected (%)")

plt.grid(True)


# Show legend

plt.legend()


# Display the plot
```

plt.show()

Conclusion

Wi-Fi routers emit **radiofrequency radiation**, which, while classified as non-ionizing and generally considered to be low-risk, may have **long-term health effects** for individuals in close proximity, such as **headaches, sleep disturbances**, and **cognitive impairments**. The **environmental impact** of these devices, including the effects on plants and soil microorganisms, also warrants further research.

Given the increasing **prevalence of Wi-Fi-enabled devices** in homes, **precautionary measures** are recommended, such as:

- **Limiting exposure** by placing routers away from sleeping areas or frequently used spaces.
- **Turning off the Wi-Fi router** at night or when not in use to minimize exposure.
- **Regulating usage time** for devices that depend on Wi-Fi for internet access.
- **Using EM shielding** or radiation-blocking technologies if concerned about EM exposure.

The cumulative effect of multiple devices emitting EM radiation, including Wi-Fi routers, requires ongoing investigation. Further research is needed to establish clearer connections between Wi-Fi radiation and potential health risks, particularly with regard to **long-term exposure** and **sensitive populations**.

This case study emphasizes the need for **greater awareness** of the potential **health risks** associated with everyday devices like Wi-Fi routers and encourages the adoption of **safer usage practices** in households.

CASE STUDY: EFFECTS OF ELECTROMAGNETIC RADIATION DUE TO LAPTOPS

Introduction

Laptops have become an indispensable tool for modern life, used for work, education, entertainment, and communication. However, the electromagnetic radiation emitted by laptops, particularly from components like **Wi-Fi antennas**, **processors**, and **batteries**, has raised concerns about potential **health effects** from long-term exposure. Laptops, like many electronic devices, emit **radiofrequency (RF) radiation**, which is a type of **non-ionizing radiation**.

This case study investigates the **biological effects** of electromagnetic radiation emitted by laptops, focusing on **human health**, **environmental impact**, and potential **electromagnetic pollution** in environments where laptops are frequently used.

Background

Laptops operate using a combination of **RF radiation** (for wireless communication), **electromagnetic fields** from the internal circuitry (such as the processor and battery), and sometimes even **magnetic fields** due to the operation of hard drives or cooling fans. While these devices are designed to be safe for typical human use, there is increasing concern about the long-term effects of constant exposure to these electromagnetic fields, especially since laptops are typically used in close proximity to the body (e.g., on a lap or near the torso).

Some potential concerns raised by **electromagnetic exposure** from laptops include:

- **Headaches** and **fatigue**
- **Sleep disturbances**
- **Cognitive impairments**
- Potential long-term risks such as **cancer** (though evidence is inconclusive)

Literature Review

Research on the effects of electromagnetic radiation from laptops has yielded mixed results. Some studies have suggested possible **health impacts**, while others have not found a clear connection. Here are a few key findings from the literature:

1. **Health Effects on Humans**:
   - **Headaches**: Individuals who spend long hours using laptops report frequent headaches.
   - **Cognitive Impairments**: Some studies have shown that continuous exposure to RF radiation might result in cognitive impairments like reduced concentration, memory issues, or difficulty processing information.
   - **Sleep Disturbances**: Research has shown that **laptop radiation**, especially from Wi-Fi connections, might interfere with sleep

patterns, particularly in individuals with **sensitivity to electromagnetic fields**.

- **Increased Risk of Cancer**: Although studies have not conclusively linked laptop radiation to cancer, some researchers suggest that prolonged exposure to RF radiation could increase the risk of certain types of cancer, particularly brain tumors.

2. **Environmental Impact**:
- **Impact on Soil and Plant Life**: Some studies suggest that electromagnetic fields could alter the growth of plants, as well as disrupt microbial life in the soil.

- **Potential Harm to Wildlife**: While much of the focus has been on human health, laptops' electromagnetic radiation could also have consequences for wildlife living in close proximity to wireless devices.

3. **Electromagnetic Hypersensitivity (EHS)**:
- Individuals suffering from **EHS** report experiencing symptoms such as dizziness, fatigue, and headaches when using laptops. However, the scientific community remains divided on the legitimacy of this condition.

Methodology

This case study employs a combination of methods to assess the effects of laptop radiation:

1. **Radiation Measurement**: Measuring the electromagnetic radiation emitted by laptops using an **RF meter** at various distances.

2. **Health Monitoring**: Collecting self-reports from individuals who regularly use laptops, noting

symptoms such as headaches, fatigue, or difficulty sleeping.

3. **Animal Studies**: Observing behavioral changes and health effects in lab animals exposed to electromagnetic radiation from laptops.

4. **Environmental Monitoring**: Studying plant growth and seed germination near areas frequently used for laptop use to assess the environmental impact.

Findings

1. Impact on Human Health

The data collected from individuals using laptops regularly suggests the following:

- **Headaches**: Many users who work or study for extended hours on laptops report frequent headaches, especially after prolonged sessions without breaks.

- **Fatigue**: Prolonged laptop use, particularly with continuous wireless communication (Wi-Fi), can cause users to experience increased feelings of tiredness and mental exhaustion.

- **Sleep Disturbances**: Exposure to RF radiation from laptops, especially when used late in the evening, is linked to difficulty falling asleep or staying asleep, particularly for individuals sensitive to EMF.

- **Cognitive Effects**: Some users report decreased concentration or memory impairment, which might be exacerbated by **blue light emissions** from the laptop screens or electromagnetic interference from the internal circuitry.

2. Impact on Animals

Studies on animals exposed to laptop EM radiation have shown:

- **Behavioral Changes**: Animals exposed to

electromagnetic radiation from laptops exhibit signs of anxiety or discomfort when placed near laptops. However, these studies remain preliminary and require further validation.

- **Health Impact**: Lab animals subjected to prolonged exposure to EM radiation have demonstrated reduced reproductive success and abnormal behavior in some studies, though results are mixed.

3. Environmental Impact

Wi-Fi-enabled laptops in areas with heavy use can potentially affect:

- **Plant Growth**: Plants placed near active laptops (or routers) show a tendency for reduced growth rates. Research has also suggested a decrease in seed germination near areas with active wireless devices.
- **Microbial Health**: There are concerns about the impact of continuous exposure to RF radiation on soil microbes. However, results are varied, and further research is needed to draw definitive conclusions.

Code to Simulate Health Impact Due to Laptop Radiation

In this simulation, we will model the relationship between **laptop radiation exposure** (measured in **$\mu W/cm^2$**) and the **percentage of individuals** reporting health issues like headaches, fatigue, and cognitive impairments.

```
import matplotlib.pyplot as plt

import numpy as np


# Data: Radiation exposure levels from laptops (µW/cm²)

exposure_levels = np.array([0, 1, 5, 10, 15, 20, 25, 30, 35, 40])


# Data: Percentage of individuals reporting health issues
```

(headaches, fatigue, sleep disturbances)

health_impact = np.array([0, 3, 6, 10, 14, 18, 22, 26, 30, 34])

```
# Create a plot
plt.figure(figsize=(8, 6))
plt.plot(exposure_levels, health_impact, marker='o', color='b', label='Health Impact')

# Add labels and title
plt.title("Effect of Laptop Radiation on Health Problems")
plt.xlabel("Radiation Exposure (µW/cm²)")
plt.ylabel("Percentage of Individuals Affected (%)")
plt.grid(True)

# Show legend
plt.legend()

# Display the plot
plt.show()
```

Conclusion

Laptops emit **radiofrequency radiation** primarily through **Wi-Fi antennas** and internal electronics. While these devices are categorized as **non-ionizing radiation** and are generally considered safe for short-term use, there are potential **long-term health effects**. The findings suggest that individuals who use laptops for extended periods may experience issues like **headaches, fatigue, sleep disturbances**, and **cognitive impairments**. Additionally, the **environmental impact** of laptop radiation, including potential effects on **plant growth** and **microbial health**, is an area requiring further investigation.

Recommendations:

1. **Use Laptops Responsibly**: Avoid prolonged use of laptops without breaks. It is recommended to take regular breaks to reduce exposure to EM radiation.

2. **Position Laptops Carefully**: Try to avoid placing laptops directly on the lap, especially during long usage sessions. Using external keyboards and mouses may help mitigate exposure.

3. **Turn Off Wi-Fi**: Turning off the laptop's Wi-Fi when not in use can significantly reduce the EM radiation exposure.

4. **Consider EMF Protection**: For individuals sensitive to electromagnetic radiation, using EMF shielding accessories, such as laptop shields or radiation-blocking cases, may help reduce exposure.

While more research is needed to definitively prove the long-term health effects of laptop radiation, taking **precautionary steps** can help reduce potential risks.

CASE STUDY: EFFECTS OF ELECTROMAGNETIC RADIATION DUE TO INDUCTION COOKTOPS

Introduction

Induction cooktops have gained popularity due to their **energy efficiency**, **faster cooking times**, and **precise temperature control**. However, they generate **electromagnetic fields (EMFs)** to heat cookware, raising concerns about their potential **health and environmental impact**. This case study explores the effects of **EM radiation** from induction cooktops on human health and surrounding environments.

Background: How Induction Cooktops Work

Unlike traditional **gas** or **electric stoves**, **induction cooktops** use **electromagnetic induction** to heat food. They generate **high-frequency alternating current (AC)** that passes through a **coil** beneath the cooktop's surface, creating a **magnetic field**. When a compatible **ferromagnetic pot** (such as cast iron or stainless steel) is placed on the cooktop, this magnetic field induces **eddy**

currents within the cookware, generating heat.

- **Frequency Range**: Induction cooktops typically operate between **20 kHz and 100 kHz**, which falls within the **radiofrequency (RF) spectrum**.

- **Magnetic Fields**: The **strength of the electromagnetic field** varies depending on the **distance from the cooktop, size of cookware**, and **power level used**.

Potential Health Concerns of Induction Cooktops

1. Human Exposure to Electromagnetic Fields (EMFs)

- **Prolonged exposure** to strong EMFs may have potential health risks.

- Induction cooktops generate **high-frequency EM radiation**, which may lead to **thermal and non-thermal effects** on the human body.

- The **World Health Organization (WHO)** and the **International Commission on Non-Ionizing Radiation Protection (ICNIRP)** have set exposure limits for EMF radiation, but concerns remain about **long-term exposure**.

2. Impact on Pregnant Women

- Studies suggest that **fetal tissues** are more sensitive to **electromagnetic fields** than adult tissues.

- Pregnant women who use induction cooktops frequently might be **more exposed** to EM radiation if they stand close to the cooktop for extended periods.

3. Effect on Medical Implants (Pacemakers & Insulin Pumps)

- The **electromagnetic fields** from induction cooktops may interfere with **implanted medical devices** like pacemakers, defibrillators, and insulin pumps.

- Some **cardiac patients** are advised to **maintain a safe distance** from induction cooktops to **avoid**

electromagnetic interference.

4. Neurological and Cognitive Effects

- Some research indicates that **prolonged EM exposure** may cause:
  - **Headaches**
  - **Fatigue**
  - **Sleep disturbances**
  - **Memory issues**
- However, the link between induction cooktops and **long-term neurological damage** is still being studied.

Environmental Impact

1. Effect on Nearby Electronics

- **Induction cooktops** can interfere with **Wi-Fi signals, mobile networks,** and **other electronic devices** operating in the same **frequency range.**

2. EM Pollution in Kitchen Environment

- Continuous use of induction cooktops contributes to **electromagnetic pollution** in enclosed spaces.
- The **intensity of EM radiation** diminishes **with distance,** but people using cooktops for extended periods may have **higher cumulative exposure.**

Experiment: Measuring EM Radiation from Induction Cooktops

To analyze the **radiation levels,** an **EMF meter** can be used to measure **electromagnetic field strength** at different distances from an induction cooktop.

Data Collection

- **Distance from cooktop** (cm): **0, 10, 20, 30, 40, 50**
- **Magnetic field strength** (in μT, microtesla): **2.5, 1.8,**

1.2, 0.7, 0.4, 0.1

Python Code: Visualizing EM Radiation Drop-Off with Distance

```python
import matplotlib.pyplot as plt
import numpy as np

# Data: Distance from induction cooktop (in cm)
distance = np.array([0, 10, 20, 30, 40, 50])

# Data: Magnetic field strength (in microtesla, µT)
magnetic_field_strength = np.array([2.5, 1.8, 1.2, 0.7, 0.4, 0.1])

# Create the plot
plt.figure(figsize=(8, 6))
plt.plot(distance, magnetic_field_strength, marker='o', color='r',
linestyle='--', label="Magnetic Field Strength")

# Add labels and title
plt.title("Electromagnetic Radiation vs. Distance from Induction
Cooktop")
plt.xlabel("Distance from Cooktop (cm)")
plt.ylabel("Magnetic Field Strength (µT)")
plt.grid(True)

# Show legend
plt.legend()

# Display the plot
plt.show()
```

Findings from EM Radiation Measurement

- **EM radiation is strongest near the cooktop** and decreases rapidly with distance.

- **At 0 cm (direct contact)**, the **magnetic field strength** is **2.5 µT**, which is relatively high.

- **At 50 cm**, the radiation drops significantly to **0.1 µT**, which is much safer.

- **Health risks are higher** for users who **stand close to the cooktop** for extended periods.

Mitigation Strategies for Reducing EM Exposure

1. Maintain a Safe Distance

- **Standing at least 30 cm away** from the induction cooktop can **significantly reduce EM exposure**.

2. Use Proper Cookware

- Use **induction-compatible cookware** made of **stainless steel** or **cast iron** to **ensure efficient heating** and **reduce stray electromagnetic fields**.

3. Avoid Prolonged Exposure

- **Limit cooking time** near the cooktop, especially for **pregnant women** or **individuals with medical implants**.

4. Turn Off Cooktop When Not in Use

- **Residual electromagnetic fields** may persist even when food is not being cooked, so it's best to **turn off the cooktop completely** after use.

5. Follow Manufacturer Safety Guidelines

- Induction cooktop manufacturers provide **safety instructions** regarding **EMF exposure**, which should be strictly followed.

Conclusion

Induction cooktops provide **fast and efficient cooking**, but they also generate **electromagnetic fields** that could pose potential **health risks**. **Prolonged exposure** may affect **neurological function, medical implants,** and **pregnant women,** while **environmental impacts** include **electromagnetic interference** with nearby devices.

Key Takeaways

Radiation intensity decreases with distance—Standing at **least 30 cm away** reduces exposure.
Pregnant women and individuals with pacemakers should use **extra caution.**
Long-term research is still needed to fully understand the **health implications.**
Simple precautions like **minimizing exposure, using proper cookware, and following safety guidelines** can reduce risks.

Future Research Directions

- Long-term studies on **the biological impact** of **induction cooktop radiation.**
- Development of **low-EMF induction cooktop technology.**
- More research on **electromagnetic pollution in kitchens** and its effects on **human health and the environment.**

www.ingramcontent.com/pod-product-compliance
Lightning Source LLC
LaVergne TN
LVHW022340060326
832902LV00022B/4149